BLUESLAND

PORTRAITS OF TWELVE MAJOR AMERICAN BLUES MASTERS

EDITED BY

Pete Welding
&
Toby Byron

A DUTTON BOOK

Dutton
Published by the Penguin Group
Penguin Books USA Inc., 375 Hudson Street,
New York, NY 10014, U.S.A.
Penguin Books Ltd, 27 Wrights Lane,
London W8 5TZ, England
Penguin Books Australia Ltd, Ringwood,
Victoria, Australia
Penguin Books Canada Ltd, 10 Alcorn Avenue,
Toronto, Ontario, Canada M4V 3B2
Penguin Books (N.Z.) Ltd, 182-190 Wairau Road,
Auckland 10, New Zealand

Penguin Books Ltd, Registered Offices:
Harmondsworth, Middlesex, England

First published by Dutton, an imprint of New American Library, a division of Penguin Books USA Inc.
Distributed in Canada by McClelland & Stewart Inc.

First Printing, December, 1991
10   9   8   7   6   5   4   3   2   1

Please turn to page 253 for additional copyright information.

 Registered Trademark—Marca Registrada

Library of Congress Cataloging-in-Publication Data

Bluesland : portraits of twelve major American blues masters /
    edited by Pete Welding and Toby Byron.
      p.   cm.
    ISBN 0-525-93375-1
    1. Blues musicians—United States—Biography.   I. Welding, Pete.
II. Byron, Toby.
ML400.B595   1991
781.643'092'273—dc20   91-14653
[B]   CIP
                                                 MN

Produced by Toby Byron/Multiprises

Printed in the United States of America
Set in Berkeley Oldstyle
Designed by Eric Baker Design Associates, Inc

For Michael Bloomfield,
and for McKinley Morganfield, Nick Gravenites,
Albert Luandrew, and Mark Adams

CONTENTS

INTRODUCTION

by William Ferris

The appearance of blues in the black community, its entry into popular American music, and its impact on black and white worlds is a fascinating tale of our time. From the first blues recording in 1920 of Mamie Smith's "That Thing Called Love" to the publication of this volume we can trace a history that establishes blues as the primary music of the twentieth century.

Our century has led us from horse-drawn vehicles to space travel, from hand-held weapons to nuclear holocaust, from a guitar heard in a single room to sounds transmitted throughout the globe. This century has borne us headlong away from life as it was known by past generations and has thrust us into a world filled with both wonder and terror. The wonder of these hundred years, which some celebrate as the dawn of a new frontier and others fear is our final time, is a music that captures both our hopes and our fears in a profound manner.

From its roots in the sacred hymns and secular work chants of slavery, blues drew on the voices of people who endured and survived conditions beyond our imagination. Slavery and the racial traumas that followed during Reconstruction and Jim Crow segregation are experiences that are forever imprinted on the historical memory of America.

Throughout the twentieth century blues has offered both black and white lives a voice of hope, and through their music they contained and overpowered evil. Whether singing about the "Big Boss Man," the Mississippi River flood of 1927, or the ghetto, blues chronicled struggle, and to this struggle it brought humor and pathos, rising like a flower in a barren field to transform lives.

As familiar today in Tokyo, Tel Aviv, and Moscow as in Itta Bena, Memphis, and Chicago, blues has bridged distant worlds of our globe as surely as technology has linked them. The music has inspired international audiences; British, French, and other audiences overseas were the first outside the black community to appreciate the blues.

Blues appeared after the Civil War as black musicians traveled in the South and developed a new music that celebrated their newfound freedom. Mobility was a central theme of the blues:

> *If anybody asks you who made up this song,*
> *Tell 'em it was _____ done been here and gone.*

Blues singers learned from work chants that were sung to coordinate heavy labor in the fields. During these chants a solo leader sang out lines, and the work crew replied in a pattern known as call and response. These work chants are a musical tradition common to both Africa and the American South and offer an important historical link between the blues and its African roots. Work chants in the South were used to coordinate tasks such as chopping wood, hoeing cotton, and laying railroad tracks. Song leaders known as gandy dancers helped railroad workers line up heavy steel tracks with verses such as:

> *Oh, talk about your pretty girl, you oughta see mine.*
> *Great big titties and a broad behind.*
> *Ha ha, way over. Ha ha, way over.*

Poor boys, pull together.
Track'll line much better
Whoa !

The black spiritual was an equally rich influence, its voicings of both hope and suffering echoed in the blues. Most blues singers grew up in the church, and hymns were an intimate part of their lives. Blues are so closely tied to hymns that singers claim they can transform a hymn into blues by substituting "My Baby" in place of "My Lord" in its verses. Blues derive much of their emotional power from the themes of spirituals and gospel music:

Motherless child sees a mighty hard time when the mother be gone.
Motherless child sees a mighty hard time when the mother be gone.
Father does the best he can, but he just don't understand.

The blues singer, too, was like a motherless child as he moved in and out of communities with his music. Loneliness strikes a familiar chord with audiences when B. B. King mixes pathos and humor through his lines:

Nobody loves me but My Momma,
And she might be jiving too.

By 1900 the blues was a familiar music in the rural South. Known as "country blues," the music was closely associated with sharecropping on cotton plantations where most blacks lived, chronicling these rural worlds in song:

I'm sitting all alone in this one-room country shack.
My woman has left me and won't be back.

As blacks migrated from the rural southern world to northern cities, they carried blues with them. Blues performers in Saint Louis and Chicago developed the boogie-woogie rhythm and used electric guitars to produce dramatic new sounds. Country blues with their moans and slower rhythms offered a musical foundation for a new sound in the cities that was known as urban blues.

During the twenties both country and urban blues performers were discovered by the recording industry, and numerous 78-rpm recordings of their songs released. Known as race records, these featured black musicians and were sold to black audiences in both the rural South and the urban North, where recording companies such as Paramount, Columbia, and Victor built an important market for their catalogs of race recordings. These early commercial records capture a rich array of male and female performers that the black community welcomed. Gussie Tobe, a Mississippi Delta musician, recalled that the impact of these records on his life was like "bringing eyesight to the blind": "I remember I had a old record player with a bulldog on it. One of them antiques, you know, that you wind. That dog would sit up there while that record was playing Bessie Smith, Blind Lemon, and all that."

In the South blues styles emerged that were associated with regions such as the Mississippi Delta, Texas, Georgia, and the Carolinas. Within each of these regional traditions performers such as Robert Johnson in the Mississippi Delta, Blind Lemon Jefferson in Texas, and Blind Willie McTell in Georgia shaped the music in distinctive ways.

Memphis and Chicago established urban blues sounds that were associated with streets famed for their blues clubs. Beale Street in Memphis and Maxwell Street in Chicago are celebrated in blues lyrics by performers who frequented these clubs.

W. C. Handy published his "The Memphis Blues or Mister Crump" in 1912. Known as the "Father of the Blues," he was the first composer to publish blues music. Handy was born in Florence, Alabama, and studied music in the classical tradition, later to discover blues while playing with his dance band in the Mississippi Delta. In Tutwiler, Mississippi, he overheard a lone musician sing "Goin' where the southern cross the Dog" and later recalled, "The singer repeated the line three times, accompanying himself on the guitar with the weirdest music I had ever heard. The tune stayed in my mind."

In 1931 Handy published forty of his compositions in his book *Blues: An Anthology*, which featured illustrations by Mexican artist Miguel Covarrubias and an important introduction by Abbe Niles. The book was an important influence on both the literary and popular music scene during the thirties.

Blues lyrics have influenced American writers throughout this century. During the thirties blues was closely identified with the jazz era. In *The Great Gatsby* F. Scott Fitzgerald's characters danced while "All night the saxophones wailed the hopeless comment of the 'Beale Street Blues.' "

Blues was an important literary form most of all for black writers associated with the Harlem Renaissance: Langston Hughes and Sterling Brown wrote blues poems, and other black writers such as Alain Locke, Claude McKay, Countee Cullen, Arna Bontemps, and Zora Neal Hurston included blues in their writing. Blues also figured prominently in the novels of black writers such as Richard Wright, Ralph Ellison, and Alice Walker. In 1973 compositions by W. C. Handy and texts of traditional blues by Robert Johnson, Leadbelly, Ma Rainey, and Blind Lemon Johnson were included in the anthology *American Literature*, edited by Robert Penn Warren, Cleanth Brooks, and R.W.B. Lewis. And Chicago poet Sterling Plumpp dedicates many of his poems to blues artists.

Blues also influenced jazz composers such as Duke Ellington, George Gershwin, and Quincy Jones, each of whom developed blues lyrics in their compositions as well as introducing blues musical techniques, such as call and response and "riffs," in their music. Flatted "blue" notes characterized performances of jazz instrumentalists such as King Oliver and Louis Armstrong, and Fletcher Henderson and Bennie Moten's jazz bands accompanied blues performers during their recording sessions and were influenced by these performances and by the growing public demand for blues.

Blues also inspired classical American composers in their work. James P. Johnson was both a fine pianist and a composer of classical piano blues such as "Snowy Morning Blues," creating a symphonic version of "Saint Louis Blues" in 1936. Aaron Copland used blues in compositions such as his 1927 Concerto for Piano and Orchestra in which he experimented with jazz; he later wrote that blues was one of the "two dominant jazz moods." Copland's First Symphony is known for its use of blues in the middle section of the scherzo.

Contemporary composer Lawrence Hoffman first performed with blues artists Skip James and Sonny Terry before earning degrees in theory and composition from the Peabody Conservatory in Baltimore. His *Blues for*

Harp, Oboe and Violoncello integrates Chicago blues from the fifties with the composer's lyric-atonal chamber music style.

The most celebrated legacy of blues in popular music is, of course, rock and roll. As one blues verse declares, "The Blues had a baby, and they named it Rock and Roll." Its king, Elvis Presley, launched his career with blues covers such as "That's All Right, Mama" by Arthur "Big Boy" Crudup and "Hound Dog" by Big Mama Thornton. Jerry Lee Lewis also drew heavily on blues in his rock and roll performances.

Interestingly, these white rock and roll artists introduced blues to white teenagers in the early fifties just as the Supreme Court's 1954 school desegregation decision was being implemented. As the civil rights movement attacked legal segregation in the United States, blues inspired a revolutionary bridge between white and black musics.

Rock and Roll was overshadowed by rock music in the sixties when British rock stars such as the Beatles and the Rolling Stones took the American music world by storm, and British musicians repeatedly acknowledged their musical debt to B. B. King and other blues artists. British rock music introduced its American fans to its blues heroes. Today B. B. King and younger artists such as Robert Cray appear regularly on MTV and other popular music programs, and contemporary white groups such as ZZ Top and black rappers such as M.C. Hammer acknowledge blues as an inspiration for their performances.

The appeal of blues to contemporary popular taste is underscored by its use in television commercials for Coca Cola and Levi's blue jeans. Once considered as a music that appealed only to a black audience, blues is now firmly established as a popular American taste.

Today blues artists perform before large audiences at annual blues festivals throughout the nation, the best known of which are the Mississippi Delta, San Francisco, Chicago, and Atlanta blues festivals. More recent annual festivals in Chunky, Mississippi, and Helena, Arkansas, draw impressive audiences and have inspired other communities that produce blues artists to recognize the music. Musicians such as B. B. King return each year to their homes in the South where they are featured in concerts.

During the past twenty years southern institutions such as the Delta Blues Museum in Clarksdale, Mississippi, the Blues Archive and *Living Blues* magazine at the University of Mississippi, and the annual Handy Blues Awards in Memphis have established important resources for blues artists. These institutions are significantly based in the region where blues began—and where for so long the music was ignored.

Blues is now receiving long overdue recognition, and the publication of *Bluesland: Portraits of Twelve Major American Blues Figures* is an important chapter in this history. Contributors are distinguished writers in the fields of blues and American music, and their portraits of blues artists are especially welcome. Far too little is known of the lives of blues performers; *Bluesland* is a tribute to the men and women who shaped the music. Through these portraits we salute the blues and its power to bring "eyesight to the blind."

William Ferris

University of Mississippi

BLIND LEMON JEFFERSON

THAT BLACK SNAKE MOAN: THE MUSIC AND MYSTERY OF BLIND LEMON JEFFERSON

by Alan Govenar

To find Blind Lemon Jefferson's grave you have to ask someone for directions. The marker, at the far end of the Wortham, Texas, cemetery on Highway 14, is easy to miss. There are no road signs leading the way. The cemetery is on an unmarked dirt road and the gravestone is an unmarked concrete slab, occupying roughly one square foot of ground. Someone has left a wreath of plastic flowers. A plaque placed by the Texas State Historical Association in 1967 identifies the grave, which itself is flat and windswept, an eerie fulfillment of Blind Lemon's plea in his 1928 song, "See That My Grave Is Kept Clean."

In the Swedish blues magazine *Jefferson,* named for the legendary singer, a caricature of Blind Lemon modeled after the only known photograph of him (a publicity still with a tie painted into the picture, reproduced as a graphic in ads for his records) appears on the inside back cover with a blurb that changes each month. In the cartoon, editor Tommy Lofgren puts words in Blind Lemon's mouth, at times ironic and poignant: "Can I change my shirt now? Is the world ready for me yet?"

Cordially Yours
Blind Lemon Jefferson

The paradox of Blind Lemon's local obscurity and the international interest in his career is nowhere more evident than in these cartoons. Despite the neglect he suffered in Texas, Blind Lemon Jefferson is celebrated as a seminal figure in the history of blues music. The stories surrounding his life and death are numerous, but are sometimes contradictory and lack solid documentation.

Although Lemon Jefferson was believed blind from birth, there is no concrete evidence; nobody seems to know for what reason he was blind or why he wore glasses, or for that matter, how he learned his way around Wortham, Kirvin, Streetman, Groesbeck, and the other small towns of East Texas, and later Dallas, Chicago, and elsewhere. It is generally accepted that Jefferson was born in 1897 to Alec and Classie Banks Jefferson in Couchman, a small community outside Wortham in Freestone County, Texas. There are no records of his receiving a formal education, and no accounts of how he learned to play the guitar although, given his singular approach to performance, it is likely that he was primarily a self-taught musician.

Quince Cox, an eighty-three-year-old black cemetery caretaker in Wortham, recalled, "Lemon started out playing his guitar on these streets and I was on those same streets. I pitched quarters and nickels to him and he'd play his guitar at any time of night. He used to play at Jake Lee's barber shop every Saturday and people came from all over to hear him play. Then he'd get on this road at ten or eleven o'clock and he'd walk to Kirvin, seven or eight miles. He'd play and keep walking, but he knew where he was going."

Alec Jefferson told Sam Charters that his mother wouldn't let him go to the country suppers where his cousin, Lemon, was playing. "They were rough. Men was hustling women and selling bootleg and Lemon was singing for them all night. They didn't even do proper kind of dancing, just stomping."

Hobart Carter, another native of the Wortham area, said that Blind Lemon's family were members of the Shiloh Baptist Church in Kirvin and that the young Jefferson was highly regarded for his abilities as a singer of spirituals as well as blues. Sam "Lightnin' " Hopkins first heard Jefferson at a Baptist church picnic in Buffalo, Texas. Eight years old at the time, Hopkins remembered watching Jefferson intently all day. Finally, he went up to the stage and tried to play along, but Jefferson was displeased and shouted, "Boy, you've got to play it right."

By this time, 1920, Jefferson was already well known in East Texas and on the streets of Dallas as both a singer and guitarist. Wortham postmaster Uel L. Davis, Jr., told reporter Laura Lippman of the Waco Tribune-Herald, "That was one thing about Lemon. He'd be singing in church one day, singing at a house of ill-repute the next."

Deep Ellum,

Dallas, 1922.

(previous overleaf)

It is unclear exactly when Blind Lemon made his first trip to Dallas (about sixty miles and sixteen train stops north of Wortham). Conflicting accounts of his early meetings with Huddie "Leadbelly" Ledbetter suggest that Blind Lemon may have been in Dallas as early as 1904. At his last recording session Leadbelly himself told producer Frederic Ramsey, Jr., that "Him (Blind Lemon) and me was singing…'round Dallas, Texas. That was in 1901, you know. Him and me was about the same age." If this is true, then Blind Lemon must have been born considerably earlier than 1897. Leadbelly was born in 1889.

Blues historian Giles Oakley wrote that the two had met in 1912 in the Deep Ellum area of Dallas (which is more likely) where they performed on the streets and traveled around Texas together. Leadbelly remarked that they were often able to get free rides on the Texas & Pacific Railroad in exchange for their playing. "I'd get Blind Lemon right on," he said. "We get out two guitars; we just ride …anything. We wouldn't have to pay no money in them times. We get on the train, the driver takes us anywhere we want to go. Well, we just get on and the conductor say, 'Boys, sit down. You goin' to play music?' We tell him, 'Yes.' " Leadbelly said that in Dallas "The women would come running, Lawd have mercy! They'd hug and kiss us so much we could hardly play. He was a blind man and I used to lead him around. When him and I go in the [train] Depot [on Central Tracks near Deep Ellum] we'd sit down and talk to one another."

Dallas's Deep Ellum was a section along Elm Street east of downtown where migrants to the city flocked. By the early 1900s Dallas had a rapidly expanding population that included African-Americans from Louisiana and the rural areas of East Texas, as well as Hispanics and Eastern European Jews. At the junction of Elm Street and Central Avenue was a railroad depot where day laborers were picked up and dropped off, taken to the cotton fields of Collin County or to other jobs. Central Avenue, which paralleled the Houston & Texas Central tracks, ran north of the central business district and connected Elm with Freedman's Town, the black neighborhood which grew up after the Civil War and branched off from Thomas and Hall Streets.

At the corner of Central Avenue and Elm Street Blind Lemon Jefferson played his guitar and sang for people who gathered to listen. Mance Lipscomb told biographer Glen Myers that "When we got to Dallas, we hung around where we could hear Blind Lemon sing and play…there were hundreds of people up and down that [Central] track. So, that's where I got acquainted with him, 1917 [the year Leadbelly was incarcerated in the prison at Huntsville for killing a man in a fight]. He hung out 'round the track, Deep Ellum. And people started coming in there, from 9:30 until six o'clock that evening, then he would go home because it was getting dark and somebody carried him home."

Lipscomb described Jefferson as a "big, loud songster... a big stout fella, and he played dance songs and never did much church song. He had a tin cup, wired on the neck of his guitar. And when you passed to give him something, why he'd thank you. But he would never take no pennies. You could drop a penny in there and he'd know the sound. He'd take and throw it away."

There are several accounts attesting to Blind Lemon's acuity in identifying the money given to him. Victoria Spivey, who knew Blind Lemon in Texas, remembered that he often used the expression "Don't play me cheap" and he meant what he said. When Blind Lemon was in Atlanta for a recording session he asked the producer, Tom Rockwell, for a five dollar advance. As a joke, Rockwell handed him a dollar bill, but Blind Lemon immediately recognized it and complained. "You could hand him a dozen bills," Tom Shaw commented. "He'd tell you just that fast whether it's a five or one dollar bill."

In familiar areas Blind Lemon's sense of direction was uncanny to those who knew him. He could usually find his way without a lead boy, but when he was traveling he welcomed help. Generally, Jefferson employed the services of young men to lead him around. Over the years, these included not only Leadbelly, but T-Bone Walker and a host of others. T-Bone Walker said, "I used to lead him around [Dallas] playing and passing the cup, take him from one beer joint to another. I liked hearing him play. He would sing like nobody's business. He was a friend of my father's. People used to crowd around him so you couldn't see him."

Josh White, who spent much of his childhood as a lead boy for blind beggars, told Paul Oliver that he took Blind Lemon into the streets around noon when the crowds were the thickest and that sometimes he even accompanied him with a tambourine, tapping a loud rhythm on his knee to draw a good crowd. Then he would turn the tambourine over and cry, "Help the blind, help the blind."

Sam Price, a blues and jazz pianist from Honey Grove, Texas, who worked at R. T. Ashford's record store and shoe-shine parlor at 408-410 North Central Avenue in Dallas, heard Blind Lemon often as he performed on the sidewalk and was instrumental in helping him to get his first recording contract. "Blind Lemon would start out from South Dallas about eleven o'clock in the morning,"

Price said, "and follow the railroad tracks to Deep Ellum, and he'd get to the corner [of Elm Street and Central Avenue] about one or two in the afternoon and he'd play guitar and sing until about ten o'clock at night. Then he'd start back home. He was a little chunky fellow who wasn't only a singer. He was a bootlegger and when he'd get back home he had such a sensitive ear. He didn't want his wife to drink. Well, when he'd go away she'd take two or three drinks out of the bottle and she'd think he didn't know it. But he'd take the bottle when he came home and say, 'Hey, how you doin' baby? How'd we do today?' 'Nobody bought no whiskey,' she'd say. Well, he'd take the bottle and shake it, and he could hear that there were two or three drinks missing. And what he'd do, he'd beat the hell out of her for that."

On the basis of Price's reports to Paramount Records, Blind Lemon Jefferson was invited to make race records in 1925. His first recordings, though not the first released, were "Old Rounder's Blues" and "Begging Back." Later in 1925, or in early 1926, under the pseudonym of Deacon L. J. Bates, he also recorded the spiritual songs "I Want To Be Like Jesus in My Heart" and "All I Want Is That Pure Religion." In February, 1926, Jefferson recorded "Got the Blues," followed in May by "Long Lonesome Blues," which became his first national hit.

Blind Lemon's guitar style was unique among the early East Texas bluesmen. He strummed or "hammered" the strings with repetitive bass figures and produced a succession of open and fretted notes, using a quick release and picking single-string arpeggios. Frequently, he took breaks in the rhythm of his songs and added extensive improvisatory passages to accentuate a word or line.

Blind Lemon's singing was loosely structured, rarely had a consistent bar structure, and usually featured his own sparse, free-form accompaniment. His voice was a high-pitched tenor, full-bodied and deeply expressive with an underlying melancholic quality resulting from his humming or moaning. He used a range of vocal techniques that enabled his singing to swell and fade, sometimes extending beyond a single octave, suspending the rhythm with a holler and holding and bending notes to emphasize his feelings and the emotions of the moment. The phrasing of his songs was often improvisatory and reflected the raw intensity with which he sang and composed his lyrics. For example, as Stephen Calt points out, "Long Lonesome Blues" begins with a $16\frac{1}{2}$ bar opening stanza, while the opening of "Black Horse Blues" has $13\frac{3}{4}$ bars, the break of "One Dime Blues" $15\frac{3}{4}$ bars, and the introduction to "Rabbit Foot Blues" has $10\frac{1}{4}$ bars that lead into a $16\frac{1}{2}$ bar verse.

Many of the songs that Blind Lemon recorded in the twenties were personalized versions of traditional folk blues from East Texas and utilized proverbs and other elements of African-American folk speech. These songs included "Jack O Diamonds," a song about the perils of gambling; a rendition of "Two Horses Standing in a Line" that he renamed "See That My Grave Is Kept Clean"; "See, See Rider," which he transformed into "Corinna Blues"; and "Boll Weevil Blues," a song-legend about the creature that devastated the cotton fields of his homeland.

In his songs Blind Lemon identified himself with the experiences of his audience—suffering and hope, economic anxiety and failure, the breakup of the family, and the desire to escape reality through wandering, love, and sex. In "Shuckin' Sugar Blues," he sang:

> I've got your picture and I'm goin' to put it in a frame
> I've got your picture and put it in a frame, shuckin' sugar
> Then if you leave town I can find you just the same

In "Sunshine Special," however, his attitude toward travel was less optimistic, even ambivalent.

> Gonna leave on the Sunshine Special, gonna leave on the Santa Fe
> Leave on the Sunshine Special, goin' in on the Santa Fe
> Don't say nothin' about that Katy
> because it's taken my brown from me

In Blind Lemon's songs travel was depicted as a means to achieve freedom and escape from the burdens of day-to-day life, but wandering also led to loneliness and separation from loved ones. This ambivalence toward "leaving" and "settling down" was a common theme in his music and was reinforced in one of his best-known songs, "Matchbox Blues."

> I'm sitting here wonderin' will a matchbox hold my clothes
> I'm sittin' here wonderin' will a matchbox hold my clothes
> I ain't got so many matches, but I got so far to go

Here again, the advantages of traveling outweighed the potential pleasures of "settling down," although the message was not completely despairing. Humor was a very important element in Blind Lemon's blues and was expounded with a wry irony, and in his songs about sexuality and sexual relations, with an almost blustering exuberance. In "Baker Shop Blues" he declared:

I'm crazy about my light bread and my pigmeat on the side
I say I'm crazy about my light bread with my pigmeat on the side
But if I taste your jellyroll I'll be satisfied
I want to know if your jellyroll is fresh,
I want to know if your jellyroll's stale
I want to know if your jellyroll is fresh,
I want to know if your jellyroll's stale
I'm gonna haul off and buy me some
if I have to break it loose in jail

Overt sexual references often were combined with humorous metaphors and analogies. In "Oil Well Blues" he underscored his own sexuality with an almost self-mocking tone:

Ain't nothin' to hurt you, sugar, ain't nothin' bad
Ain't nothin' to hurt you, honey, ain't nothin' bad
It's the first oil well that your little boy ever had

In his "That Black Snake Moan" songs Blind Lemon was even more obvious in his sexual allusions and in so doing accentuated his own lascivious sense of humor.

Mmmm-mm, black snake crawlin' in my room
Mmmm-mm, black snake crawlin' in my room
Some pretty mama better come
and get this black snake soon

Then, in "That Black Snake Moan, No. 2," he reiterated his desires with greater emphasis:

I woke up this morning, black snake was
makin' such a ruckus in my room
Black snake is evil, black snake is all I see
Black snake is evil, black snake is all I see
woke up this morning, black snake was moved in on me

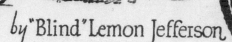

In contrast to Blind Lemon's scurrilous sexual humor were his ambivalent feelings about women. In some of his songs women were called "good gal," "sugar," "baby," "honey," and "high brown," but in others they were scorned as "wild," "dirty mistreaters," and "deceitful."

In "Elder Green" Blind Lemon expressed his attraction for his woman with enthusiasm.

> *I've got a high brown and she's long and tall*
> *Lord, Lord, Lord, she'll make a panther squall*

In "Got the Blues," however, he is both intrigued and repulsed by his "good gal."

> *You can't ever tell what a woman's got on her mind*
> *Man, you can't tell what a woman's got on her mind*
> *You might think she's crazy about you*
> *she's leaving you all the time*

In "Piney Woods Money Mama" his antagonism is provoked by a conniving mother.

Elm Street theaters,

Dallas,1925.

(following overleaf)

> *Lord, heavy hip mama, she done moved to this Piney Wood*
> *Heavy hip mama, she done moved to this Piney Wood*
> *She's a high steppin' woman she don't mean no man no good*
> *She got ways like the devil*
> *and hair like an Indian squaw*
> *She got ways like the devil*
> *and hair like an Indian squaw*
> *She's been tryin' two years*
> *to get me to be her son-in-law*

In general, the women in Blind Lemon's songs were revered for their sexuality and allure, but were also condemned for their withheld love and manipulative personalities. In "Pneumonia Blues" he held his woman responsible for his illness; in "Prison Cell Blues," for his incarceration; in "Deceitful Brownskin Blues," for robbing him; and in "Peach Orchard Mama," for cheating on him.

The details of Blind Lemon's actual relationships with women during his adult life are sketchy. Pianist Sam Price said that he married a young woman named Roberta from his "home state" in the early twenties and that they had a child together soon thereafter, although there are no records of the child's name or date of birth or what ultimately happened to his alleged wife.

By casting women into such a wide range of roles in his songs, Blind Lemon was able to identify more fully with the experiences of his audience. This identification not only concerned relations with women, but carried into other areas of life and suffering. In "Mosquito Moan" Blind Lemon recounted the displeasures caused by a common insect, but retained his sense of humor.

> *Now I'm sittin' in my kitchen, mosquitoes all around my screen*
> *Now I'm sittin' in my kitchen, mosquitoes all around my screen*
> *If I don't arrange to get a mosquito bomb, I'll be seldom seen*

In his songs Blind Lemon talked about many of the pests and animals found in East Texas farming communities, including mules, cows, horses, snakes, and rabbits. Animals were a means of conveying a sense of time and place, but were also used as allusions to travel, sexuality, and despair.

HOTEL
SARATOGA
CAFÉ
HOTEL
CRISWELL
DALLAS
HARDWARE
COMPANY

MAJESTIC
BIG TIME VAUDEVILLE
FRANK VAN HOVEN
MINSTRELMONARCH
M DIAMOND & CO
MCFARLAN PALACE
MELBA
MELBA THEATRE
MAJESTIC THEATRE BUILDING

In "One Dime Blues," "Broke and Hungry," and "Tin Cup Blues" Blind Lemon commented poignantly on the conditions of poverty and oppression that were rampant among African-Americans. In "Tin Cup Blues," he lamented:

> I stood on the corner and almost bust my head
> I stood on the corner, almost bust my head
> I couldn't earn enough to buy me a loaf of bread
> My gal's a housemaid and she earns a dollar a week
> I said, my gal's a housemaid and she earns a dollar a week
> I'm so hungry on payday, I can hardly speak
> Now gather round me, people, let me tell you a true fact
> I said, gather round me, people, let me tell you a true fact
> That tough luck has stuck me and the rats is sleepin' in my hat

In addition to the personal hardships of his audience, Blind Lemon sang about the ravages of natural disaster—flood—in "Rising High Water Blues" and—although there were no records of him having spent time in jail—about the injustices of the criminal justice system. In "Hangman's Blues" Blind Lemon demonstrated his ability to project himself into another man's fear and anxiety.

> Well, mean old hangman is waitin' to tighten up that noose
> I have a mean old hangman waitin' to tighten up that noose
> Lord, I'm so scared I am tremblin' in my shoes
> Jury heard my case and said my hands was red
> Jury heard my case and said my hands was red
> And judge he sentenced me to be hangin' till I'm dead
> The crowd is around the courthouse and time is goin' fast
> And the crowd is around the courthouse and time is goin' fast
> Soon a good-for-nothin' killer is goin' to breathe his last

Blind Lemon recorded two versions of this song; the earlier, more dramatic version's fast, pulsating guitar accompaniment was perhaps meant to simulate the rapid heartbeat of the convicted man. In "Hangman's Blues," as well as in "Prison Cell Blues," " 'Lectric Chair Blues," "Lockstep Blues," and "Blind Lemon's Penitentiary Blues," he depicted jail life as grim and cruel. He sympathized with the incarcerated inmates and criticized the unfairness of the court system. Blind Lemon's songs about prison and the longing for freedom were not his most popular, but they nonetheless reflected the social conditions of the times and represented themes vital to the country blues tradition.

From 1926 to 1928 Blind Lemon proved to be the most successful country blues singer in the United States. During this period he commuted frequently between Dallas and Chicago, where he had a South Side "kitchenette" at Thirty-seventh and Rhodes, and continued to travel around Texas and to other states, including Oklahoma, Georgia, and Mississippi. Mississippi Delta bluesman Houston Stackhouse remembered seeing Jefferson in his hometown. "He came to Crystal Springs and was playin' in some little show for a doctor. They had it in Freetown there at the colored school. There was plenty of people there. It was a big school and crowded all indoors, people couldn't get to see him. They had to bring him out to the front, on the porch."

Blind Lemon's producer for Paramount records, Mayo Williams, marveled at the appeal of his songs. In an interview with Stephen Calt, Williams commented that "He [Blind Lemon] was a soul singer naturally," though he doubted that he could have originated all of his song themes. "He was just as cool and calm and collected," he said, "as any artist I've ever seen." In appreciation of Blind Lemon's earning power, Williams bought him a $725 Ford, which the singer hired a chauffeur to drive for him. Blind Lemon also owned a 1923 or 1924 Dodge that he was reported to have talked about in his performances. According to Williams, Blind Lemon's royalties accumulated so quickly that he was encouraged to open a savings account, which reached a balance of $1,500.

By 1929 interest in Blind Lemon's music began to decline. His instrumental arrangements became more derivative of his earlier work and the enthusiasm which he brought to the recording studio deteriorated.

Nonetheless, when he died in December of 1929 the circumstances were inscrutable. No official record of his death has been found and the oral accounts are somewhat contradictory. Arthur Laibly, who succeeded Mayo Williams as Jefferson's producer, said (on the basis of a report from his office assistant) that Blind Lemon died of a heart attack. Laibly heard that Blind Lemon died during a blizzard, a fact which was later substantiated by Williams, who added that he had collapsed in his car and was abandoned by his chauffeur.

When asked about his funeral, Wortham cemetery caretaker Quince Cox was quick to reply. "Anyone over the age of sixty remembers that day well," he said in a hoarse voice. "They brought his body back to Texas by train. People said he died in the snow after a recording session in Chicago, that he was lost, couldn't find his way. Some thought it was foul play. Two or three hundred people came to the funeral, black and white, to watch his coffin lowered into the ground."

Charley Patton,

the first blues great

at the beginning of

the century.

Within six months of Blind Lemon's death Paramount attempted to capitalize on his tragic misfortune by issuing six posthumous records, the last—intended as a two-sided tribute to him—recorded in the summer of 1930. Laibly tried to persuade Charlie Patton and Son House to sing tributes. Both had recently recorded for Paramount, and as it turned out, the tribute by House was not labeled as such. Instead, Paramount issued a recording of a sermon delivered by Reverend Emmet Dickenson entitled "Death of Blind Lemon," which eulogized the singer with a religious fervor:

LET US PAUSE FOR A MOMENT AND THINK OF THE LIFE OF OUR BELOVED BLIND LEMON JEFFERSON WHO WAS BORN BLIND. IT IS IN MANY RESPECTS LIKE THAT OF OUR LORD, JESUS CHRIST. LIKE HIM, UNTO THE AGE OF THIRTY HE WAS UNKNOWN, AND ALSO LIKE HIM IN THE SPACE OF A LITTLE OVER THREE YEARS THIS MAN AND HIS WORKS WERE IN EVERY HOME. I BELIEVE THAT THE LORD IN BLIND LEMON HAS SOWN A NATURAL BODY AND WILL RAISE IT A SPIRITUAL BODY. WHEN I WAS INFORMED OF LEMON'S DEATH, I THOUGHT OF OUR LORD JESUS CHRIST AS HE WALKED DOWN THE JERICHO ROAD AND SAW A MAN WHO WAS BORN BLIND. AND HIS DISCIPLES SAID, "MASTER, WHO DID SIN? DID THIS MAN SIN OR HIS PARENTS, THAT HE IS A MAN BORN BLIND?" AND JESUS CHRIST ANSWERED, "NEITHER DID THIS MAN SIN NOR HIS PARENTS SIN BUT THAT I MAY BE MANIFESTED IN HIM." LEMON JEFFERSON WAS BORN BLIND AND WAS CUT OFF FROM THE GOOD THINGS OF THIS LIFE THAT YOU AND I MIGHT ENJOY; HE TRULY HAD A CROSS TO BEAR. HOW MANY OF US TODAY ARE CRYING ABOUT THE CROSSES WE ARE TO BEAR: "OH LORD, THIS IS TOO HARD FOR ME; OH LORD, MY LIFE IS MISERABLE TO LEAD." BLIND LEMON IS DEAD. AS LEMON DIED WITH THE LORD, SO DID HE LIVE.

Indicative of the esteem and commercial import of Blind Lemon Jefferson is this recording that was written for him.

If Reverend Dickenson's sermon did little to explain the reality of Blind Lemon's life and death, it was nevertheless testimony to the magnitude of his career and its importance in African-American culture during the twenties. Over a period of roughly four years, Blind Lemon made eighty-nine recordings. In these he exhibited his virtuosity as a singer and guitarist who had a profound influence upon the musicians of his generation and upon the development of country blues. In his music Blind Lemon combined traditional themes with autobiographical and historical details at once erotic and humorous, ironic and grim: the intensity of his music reflected the immediacy and determination with which he lived.

LONNIE JOHNSON

CHASED BY THE BLUES

by Chris Albertson

Over the years, jazz writers have shown a tendency to turn somewhat morbid when dealing with blues singers. If the gloom wasn't there, they often invented it—God forbid that a singer of sad songs should lead a happy life. This is not to say that Lonnie Johnson's was a bowl of cherries, but neither were things as hopeless as Samuel Charters pictured them in his 1959 book *Country Blues*. A chapter devoted to Lonnie had him living in Cincinnati that year, "not well, and doing very little musically." It described him as a sad person who had gone through life as a loner and become "a sick man, shabbily dressed," too ashamed to show his face. "For Lonnie," read the tear-wrenching summation, "it has been a long road, without much of an end."

It had, indeed, been a long road, but one paved with triumph as well as tragedy, and it was far from over. In 1958, when I had a daily show on Philadelphia jazz station WHAT-FM, Lonnie's records frequently graced my turntables. I had always admired his versatility, and I relished treating my listeners

to the breadth of his artistry: the superb plaintive blues, the racy double entendre duets with Victoria Spivey and Spencer Williams, the pioneering instrumental duets with guitarist Eddie Lang, and his dazzling guitar solos on classic Armstrong and Ellington sides. Lonnie Johnson was an outstanding blues artist and composer, but his influence stretched far beyond the idiom with which he was most closely identified; his intricate twelve-string guitar work of the twenties is the foundation for much of the music we hear today.

Being a recent immigrant from Denmark—where the government-operated radio afforded jazz as much reverence as it did any other important art forms—I was astonished to find that Lonnie Johnson's name was unfamiliar to many of my American listeners, even those who considered themselves to be dedicated jazz fans. The few who had heard of him, knew only of his commercial hits, songs like "He's a Jelly Roll Baker" and "Tomorrow Night," and I was determined to set the record straight, as it were. One morning, after playing some of his wonderful twenties sides, I wondered aloud what had happened to Lonnie Johnson, and the phone instantly lit up. The first caller was banjo player and former bandleader Elmer Snowden—then a parking lot attendant—who himself was a legendary figure, having introduced Duke Ellington to Harlem in 1922. Elmer reported that Lonnie had lived in Philadelphia for the past several years, and that he had seen him at a local supermarket the day before—so much for being down and out in Cincinnati. The next call came from a gentleman who worked at the Benjamin Franklin Hotel and had a coworker named Lonnie Johnson, but he knew nothing of this man, a janitor, having a more glamorous past.

That afternoon, the hotel's maintenance supervisor said he thought it unlikely that Johnson was a famous performer, but added "he might play guitar, because he's real careful with his hands, and always wears gloves to protect them." Indeed he did, and I recognized Lonnie Johnson instantly as he reported for his three-to-midnight shift that day.

The following Saturday afternoon, I arranged a small gathering at my apartment for the purpose of bringing Lonnie and Elmer to the attention of two top New York record producers who had accepted my invitation to come down. I had neither met nor spoken to John Hammond and Orrin Keepnews before, but the mere fact that they made the trip and seemed eager to hear Lonnie and Elmer gave me hope. I still have my tapes from that gathering, so I don't rely on memory when I report that it was an evening filled with amazing music. Lonnie, this lean man with a misleading, perpetually sad face, looked much younger than his years. That afternoon, he was in a splendid mood as he exchanged stories with Elmer, a jolly, slightly overweight man who seemed to accept second billing. There were many questions and compliments from Hammond and Keepnews—who represented Columbia and Riverside Records, respectively—but neither man seemed prepared to whisk anyone into a recording studio. A few days later, I took the tapes to Bob Weinstock, the owner of Prestige Records, who immediately approved the recording of an "exploratory" Lonnie Johnson album. A month later, when he heard the test pressing of *Blues by Lonnie Johnson*, Weinstock was so impressed that he signed Lonnie to a contract. Several albums followed, including *Blues and Ballads*, featuring Lonnie and Elmer together, and one that reunited Lonnie with an old studio partner from the twenties, Victoria Spivey. Lonnie's career was once again heading up.

Encouraged by Weinstock's reaction, and egged on by the kind of boldness that can only come from naïveté, I picked up the phone and called the William Morris Agency. As it happened, my call was routed to a devoted Lonnie Johnson fan who was delighted to hear that he was alive, well, and available. The result was a one-month booking at Chicago's Playboy Club, at $350 per week. I told Lonnie that I did not intend to make money on him, but that I expected to eventually be reimbursed for my expenses, which now included a tuxedo and a Gibson guitar. As it turned out, I was repaid a total of $25, but it was impossible to get angry with Lonnie; he had a way of looking as sad as his most poignant songs, and to know his background was to understand his fear of hitting the skids again. I understood that those who handled Lonnie's business matters in the past had not always done so honestly, so it was not surprising to find that he viewed my offer of nonprofit management with suspicion. In some ways, Lonnie was out to get back some of the losses he had suffered at the hands of shady managers, club owners, and record company powers, but it was clear that he also bore some blame for past slides.

This, the last in a series of comebacks, happened to be perfectly timed. America was experiencing a folk music revival that embraced ersatz "folkies" like the Kingston Trio, Bob Gibson, Oscar Brand, and Peter, Paul and Mary, but also focused renewed attention on the real thing, including the blues singers of the twenties. Young folk music fans were eager to learn more about men and women whose names appeared on time-worn 78-rpm record labels, and among them few performers had recorded as prolifically as Lonnie Johnson.

As his name began to appear in newspapers, and his records were played on the air, Lonnie basked in his newfound celebrity status. Unlike previous peaks he had experienced, the crowds that now gathered around him consisted mainly of young white fans who were perhaps more attracted by the mystique of a legend stepping out of history than by anything he sang or played. They were full of questions about the artists he had worked with and about his own past, but Lonnie had few answers; there were times when all the attention seemed to overwhelm him, and while he responded politely to fans and press people, he hardly ever volunteered personal information. Even I found him reluctant to discuss his past, except to acknowledge that which had already been written.

Born Alonzo Johnson, in New Orleans, he often gave his birth date as February 8, 1900, but one night he inadvertently told me that it was 1894; other years have been mentioned, but a youthful demeanor and some quick calculation made '94 seem quite plausible. He was one of thirteen children, all of whom were groomed to play in their father's string ensemble. "There was music all around us," Lonnie recalled, "and in my family you'd better play something, even if you just banged on a tin can." His first instrument was the violin, then the guitar, bass, and piano, but singing did not occur to him. "I just didn't think of it, not until much later, because me and my brother was doing alright with our instruments, and those joints we played in didn't particularly want any vocals." He was still a teenager when he began earning money as a violinist, playing in many of the city's cafés with one of his brothers, James "Steady Roll" Johnson. "We played anything they wanted to hear," he said, "ragtime melodies, sweet songs, waltzes—that kind of thing. A lot of people liked opera, so we did some of that, too." In the early part of the century, New Orleans was a melting pot of musical cultures; jazz, as we would come to know it, was beginning to rattle spittoons and set bodies in motion at some of the city's less respectable establishments, and it thrived in Storyville, the red light district. Lonnie loved the diversity of sounds, and soon found his way into some of the area's hottest bands, but his performance was still too ordinary to make an impression.

In 1917, as the country entered World War I and the U.S. Navy shut down Storyville, Lonnie sailed for London with a musical revue about which no details have been unearthed. He himself had little to say about this production, focusing instead on the devastating news that greeted him upon his return to New Orleans: virtually his entire family had been wiped out by the widespread influenza epidemic of 1918. With the family gone—except for his brother, James—and Storyville closed down, Lonnie joined the northern migration. He spent much of the postwar period playing on Mississippi riverboats, including stints with Charlie Creath's Jazz-O-Maniacs on the SS *St. Paul* and Fate Marable's SS *Capitol* band. The Johnson brothers were now living in Saint Louis, and Lonnie had become an experienced performer of remarkable versatility and imagination. Still, there was not enough steady work in the music field, so, for close to two years, he toiled in a steel foundry by day.

The country—indeed, the Western world—was undergoing a major change as Europe recovered from the war. The artistic community was forging new ground on all fronts, and the shackles of Victorianism were gleefully broken by hedonistic flappers. The more conservative crowd welcomed Prohibition—which banned the sale and consumption of alcoholic beverages in America—but the fun-seekers saw it as a challenge. Speakeasies could be found everywhere, and hip flasks were as common as Arrow collars. Painters and dancers broke with convention, shunned romanticism, and gave the world a new perspective; so did composers like Stravinsky, Schönberg, and Bartók, but perhaps the most radical departure came from Black America. Jazz was not wholly the product of New Orleans, but the Crescent City was clearly a wellspring from which had emerged some of the idiom's greatest early forces. By 1925, when Lonnie stood in the wings, ready to make his most consequential move, records by King Oliver, Louis Armstrong, Duke Ellington, Fletcher Henderson, and Bessie Smith were already spinning their magic on Victrolas throughout the world. Europeans were particularly excited by "le jazz hot," which fit right into the world's changing, more venturesome pattern—it was decidedly the beat to which the decade stepped. Of course, like any new, unorthodox art form, jazz and blues had its detractors, stiff-collared spoilsports who saw it as the devil's music, designed to arouse "animal passions."

Lonnie knew that he would have to make records in order to be noticed beyond Saint Louis, which is why he entered a blues contest at the city's Booker T. Washington Theater. The blues craze was at its height, and the first prize was an OKeh recording contract. "I had done some singing by then," he recalled, "but I still didn't take it as seriously as my guitar playing, and I guess I would have done anything to get recorded—it just happened to be a blues contest, so I sang the blues." It also happened to be Lonnie Johnson's ticket to stardom. The contest ran for eight weeks before Lonnie was declared the winner, and OKeh wasted no time getting him into the studio. A couple of months later, in January, 1926, Lonnie's first coupling, "Mr. Johnson's Blues" and "Falling Rain Blues," was shipped to the country's race record shops.

It was well received, and by the end of January Lonnie had recorded nine additional sides on his own, and participated on one other, by Charlie Creath's band. Clearly, this was no ordinary artist; he was far more polished than the day's male blues singers, and his extraordinary instrumental skills matched

Big Bill Broonzy,

a pacesetting musician.

Along with Lonnie

Johnson he was one

of the leading

singer/guitarists and

all around session

players in Chicago

in the thirties.

(facing page)

those of the era's leading jazz players. Consequently, Lonnie began performing along the RKO and TOBA theater circuits, outlets that remained closed to such contemporary country blues artists as Blind Lemon Jefferson, Papa Charlie Jackson, and Blind Blake.

Although he was signed as a blues singer, Lonnie's versatility did not escape the producers at OKeh, who hired him as a staff musician and teamed him up with some of the label's hottest artists. Thus Lonnie made prominent guest appearances on OKeh recordings by the Chocolate Dandies, Louis Armstrong, and Duke Ellington, greatly enhancing sides like the Armstrong Hot Five's "I'm Not Rough" and "Hotter Than That," and Duke's "The Mooche" and "Hot and Bothered." These recordings have since become classics, largely due to Lonnie's dizzying guitar solos. In 1928 and 1929, OKeh teamed Lonnie up with guitarist Eddie Lang for a series of superb duets, but Lang—a white man whose real name was Salvatore Massaro, and who later became Bing Crosby's accompanist—was listed on the labels as "Blind Willie Dunn." The public, or so OKeh believed, was not ready for mixed bands.

On his own and as accompanist to singers ranging from Clara Smith and Bertha Chippie Hill to Martha Raye, Lonnie made over two hundred recordings during the two decades that followed his contest victory, but because he enjoyed such success as a singer and songwriter his instrumental talent often was overlooked. Actually, Lonnie would have been assured a prominent spot in jazz history even if he had never sung a word. As a guitarist, he was way ahead of his time, a brilliant, imaginative player whose dexterous technique and advanced ideas had great effect on many of his illustrious contemporaries and on generations of musicians to come.

Lonnie's urban blues style profoundly affected such contemporaries of his as Big Bill Broonzy, but today's generation of blues fans also can hear his ideas echoed in the work of current stars like B. B. King. But the sphere of Lonnie's influence reached beyond individual musicians to the music itself; his introduction to jazz of single-line countermelodies deeply influenced the work of such younger men as Charlie Christian and Django Reinhardt, and set the course for much of today's music.

Although he wrote hundreds of compelling blues lyrics and probably was best known as a blues artist, Lonnie wanted desperately to make his mark as a ballad singer. The few times he ever requested I play a record for him,

he asked to hear Frank Sinatra or Nat King Cole. In 1960 I arranged to have him
included in the all-star lineup of a folk music concert at New York's Town Hall. The
day's most popular folkies were on hand, and the idea was to have Lonnie represent
the blues. "Be sure you sing a blues," I told him, knowing full well that he would
prefer to deliver some romantic pop song. "I will, I will," he replied, nodding his
head vigorously, but when the time came, he stepped up to the microphone and
dedicated the song to me "for making his appearance possible"—then he sang Frank

Sinatra's hit, "This Love of Mine." I could almost feel the crowd's disappointment as this legendary blues man, in a sense, betrayed them. At first I became angry, but then I realized that there was a message in Lonnie's song: that we shouldn't paint artists into corners, and that it doesn't really matter who wrote a song or where it came from, as long as it stirs us. Lonnie's eloquent rendering of "This Love of Mine" was as gripping as any blues I had ever heard him sing, and when he was through the audience's disappointment had turned to enthusiasm. Lonnie had proved his point, and I never again insisted that he sing a blues—I did, however, once ask him to compose a blues. It happened during the early days of our friendship; an advertising agency, having heard Lonnie perform on my radio show, asked me if he could write a one-minute blues to be used as a commercial for an auto insurance company. When I handed Lonnie a fact sheet with all the information they wanted included, he looked at it, said "Okay," and disappeared into the next room. A half hour later he returned and performed for me a blues that lasted exactly one minute and contained all the facts I had given him—and it all rhymed perfectly.

A superb lyric writer who preferred to sing his own songs, Lonnie rarely resorted to clichés, but his melodic compositions offered less variety. "I play the same on a lot of my recordings," he said, candidly, "but most people don't realize it, because my stories are not the same, and people usually don't pay no attention to chords."

Toward the end of the thirties, Lonnie toured with Bessie Smith's *Midnight Steppers* show, traveling in her private railroad car. By all accounts, he was the only blues singer with whom Bessie shared a bill, and that was not all she shared. "I used to see him tiptoe into Bessie's state room at night, and I would try to keep awake so that I could see how long he stayed there," said Bessie's niece, Ruby Walker, who was one of the show's chorines, "but I always fell asleep before he came out."

In 1932, Lonnie had left OKeh—which had been absorbed by Columbia Records in 1926—and moved to Cleveland. The Great Depression was in full bloom, the theater circuits had all but abandoned live shows in favor of the "talkies," and the recording industry's outlook was bleak. He took whatever playing jobs he could get, including occasional work with Putney Dandridge's orchestra, but found himself once again forced into factory work. Had he handled his money more prudently, Lonnie might have continued his music career without interruption, but his lifestyle embraced flashy clothes and pampered girlfriends, so there never seemed to be any money left over for that rainy day.

(Thirty years later, Lonnie hadn't changed: he now worked hard to hide his advancing years, to sate his appetite for young women, and to give the appearance of solvency. Since it took more money than he usually had to attract his partners of choice, he was ever thinking up ways to fatten his wallet and, to that end, he called Prestige Records producer Esmond Edwards three times in six months to request an advance on his next album, because his house had burned down. When the fourth call came, Edwards caught on.)

Lonnie did not record between 1932 and 1937, but then came a bid from Decca, followed, in 1939, by a Bluebird contract that yielded a wealth of excellent sides, including "He's a Jelly Roll Baker," his first rhythm and blues hit. By the early to mid-forties, Lonnie's career was going well again, due to the popularity of rhythm and blues—which was based on the kind of music Lonnie had been playing for over twenty years—and, in part, to a jazz renaissance that had collectors scouring the country's attics for forgotten recordings and scurrying to bring back alive some of the legendary figures of traditional jazz. A Decca recording project featured him with an all-star group of New Orleans veterans—including clarinetist Johnny Dodds, his brother drummer Baby Dodds, and trumpeter Natty Dominique—and he became a frequent guest on radio broadcasts aimed at the so-called "moldy fig," a tag given to dyed-in-the-wool fans of traditional New Orleans jazz. Lonnie went along with such nostalgic events, but he felt that he had outgrown the sounds of the past, and it was time to concentrate on the kind of music that could truly fatten the wallet. Under contract to King Records, a Cincinnati-based rhythm and blues label, he scored a pop hit in 1947 with "Tomorrow Night," and followed it up the next year with an even bigger single, "Pleasing You." While his rhythm and blues hits focused renewed attention on him, Lonnie couldn't escape the past, which is what brought him to England in 1952, at the height of Europe's "Trad" fever. Spearheaded by such English traditionalists as Humphrey Lyttelton, Chris Barber, Mick Mulligan, and Ken Colyer, young European jazz fans flocked to hear the sounds of old New Orleans imitated by local musicians who replicated every note, including the sour ones. The genuine article, like Lonnie Johnson, was a rare treat, and many an old, forgotten jazz and blues figure was suddenly given movie star status in the cellar joints of Europe.

Unfortunately, the Trad euphoria didn't last, and when the party was over in Europe, men like Lonnie found themselves returning to the bleak reality that often faces the has-been star. That brings us back to 1960 and Philadelphia's Benjamin Franklin Hotel. Around the time of Lonnie's appearance at the folk concert, I read that the Duke Ellington Orchestra was also going to be

Lonnie Johnson,

pictured with

Barney Bigard,

clarinet; Rex Stewart,

cornet; and Truck

Parham, bass, was

among the few

bluesmen of the late

twenties and thirties

to work well

with jazz figures.

(following overleaf)

47

performing at Town Hall, so I called the producer and suggested a reunion. He liked the idea and the deal was made—Lonnie would be featured as soloist on one number, and it would be just like the old days. It wasn't. Lonnie was nervous, and we were both upset by a headline that appeared in the *New York Daily News* that day: "The Janitor Meets the Duke." Even when his career was at its lowest, Lonnie Johnson maintained his dignity, and there was nothing cute about a headline that exploited his misfortune. The real reason why this brief reunion didn't produce memorable music was distance—Town Hall, 1960, was simply too far removed from the 1928 Columbia studio that sparked Lonnie and Duke's first collaboration. This was a different Ellington band and Lonnie's playing had changed a great deal; the sound of his electric guitar was conventional by comparison with the richly-textured twelve-string instrument that ignited the old versions of "Hot and Bothered" and, especially, "The Mooche."

Shortly after his return from the Chicago Playboy Club engagement, Lonnie was able to quit his job at the Benjamin Franklin. He spent the early sixties working a busy schedule that took him to Europe on more than one occasion, and to folk festivals around the country. He also made records in England, Denmark, and Germany, and—obviously to cash in on his revitalized career—King reissued a single of "Tomorrow Night," only this time with a silly background of doo-wahs, complete with a one-note piano accompaniment. Lonnie's voice was all but drowned out in this nightmarish overdub, and he cried when I played him the record.

The last time I saw Lonnie was around 1965; he was seated at the bar of a Greenwich Village night spot, signing autographs for a group of young fans, but times had changed again: the Beatles had made their appearance, European fans were tuned in to rock music, and the folk music fad was history. Lonnie spotted me as he looked over the heads of his admirers, but he said nothing. A few weeks later, he called to tell me that he had an idea that could make both of us some money, but I declined the offer, feeling that I had done my part. Shortly thereafter, Lonnie moved to Toronto, Canada, where he spent his remaining years performing in local clubs. Lonnie was afraid of cars, but in 1969 he was struck by one as it jumped a sidewalk in a freak accident. He never fully recovered, and died June 16, 1970, of a related stroke.

T'AINT NOBODY'S
BUSINESS IF I DO

by Chris Albertson

They sang blues tunes, but the majority of the twenties blues "queens" actually were so-called "sweet singers" and vaudeville artists who recognized a lucrative trend when they heard it. The blues craze that swept the Eastern half of the country in the twenties started with the release and overwhelming success of Mamie Smith's 1920 OKeh recording, "Crazy Blues." Mamie Smith's debut record had not done very well, but this one—an uninteresting composition sung in a rather ordinary style—had cash registers ringing in the most unlikely places. The burgeoning record industry's decision makers put on their thinking caps: what they had was a black singer and band doing a twelve-bar blues number—who was buying it in such numbers? Could it be that "Negroes" actually bought phonograph records? What an odd thought. Stranger yet, could it be that white people bought "colored" music performed by "colored" artists? No, that one was too far out, so they pondered further and realized that they had made an extraordinary discovery: black people wanted black music on their phonographs. It was time to load up and take aim.

Soon, big and small record companies started scouting around for blues ladies, and a new category of music was added to record catalogs: "race records." By 1923, the bigger companies had gone so far as to establish race divisions, and the segregation was extended to the retail level where race records were sold through race record shops of which every major city with a sizeable black population had at least one. Several smaller labels were formed to record black music exclusively; one of them, Black Swan—owned by two black men, composer W. C. Handy and his partner in the music publishing business, Harry Pace— boasted in its advertisements: "The Only Genuinely Colored Record, Others Are Only Passing."

As companies sought to tap this newfound market, many singers who had been knocking around in chorus lines suddenly found themselves with recording contracts. Some were quite good, but most of them had bland, indistinguishable voices. Today, certain recordings by the period's most atrocious singers survive only because they feature extraordinary accompaniments. But the period also produced a wealth of fine vocal performances, and none are more enduring than the 160 sides left us by Bessie Smith, whose exceptional talent would have taken her to the top with or without a blues craze. Still, the blues idiom suited her style particularly well. "I don't ever remember any artist in my long, long years who could evoke the response from her listeners that Bessie Smith did," said the late Frank Schiffman, owner of Harlem's Lafayette and Apollo theaters where Bessie performed at early and late stages of her career. "Whatever pathos there is in the world, whatever sadness she had, was brought out in her singing—and the audience knew it and responded to it."

"When it came to singing the blues, no one could touch Bessie," said singer-dancer Mae Barnes, "in fact, she could sing just about anything and make you listen." For promotional purposes, Bessie was named "Queen of the Blues," but the tag became such a common appellation for female blues singers that someone changed Bessie's to "Empress of the Blues," and it remained exclusively with her.

There was indeed something majestic about Bessie, and confirmation of that came right from Windsor Castle. "The Prince of Wales was showing us around, and we came to a huge portrait of Queen Mary," said Ms. Barnes as she reminisced about a thirties guided tour of the royal home. 'What a regal woman,' I said. He nodded and said 'Yes, I believe there are only two truly regal women in this world, my mother and Bessie Smith.'"

In 1921, when "Crazy Blues" was selling at the rate of over seven thousand copies per week, Bessie Smith was already a seasoned performer, steeped in the blues and well known to audiences throughout the South. Born in the Blue Goose Hollow section, at the foot of Chattanooga, Tennessee's, Cameron Hill, her first home was a weather-beaten, dilapidated one-room cabin which she shared with her parents and six brothers and sisters. No official record of her birth exists, but the date was probably April 15, 1894. When both parents died, Viola, Bessie's oldest sister, became the family head, but her income from taking in laundry was a meager one, so everybody who was big enough pitched in. Bessie and her brother Andrew took to the streets, where she sang and danced to his guitar accompaniments. "She used to sing 'Bill Bailey, Won't You Please Come Home?' " recalled Will Johnson, who often saw the duo perform in front of the White Elephant Saloon on Thirteenth and Elm, "and whenever someone threw a fat coin her way, she'd say something like 'That's right, Charlie, *give* to the church.' I always thought she had more talent as a performer—you know, dancing and clowning—than as a singer, at least in those days I don't remember being particularly impressed with her voice. She sure knew how to shake money loose from a pocket, though."

Bessie looked up to her oldest brother, Clarence, who worked at odd jobs but had loftier aspirations. When you live in abject poverty, surrounded by more of the same, even the tackiest little entertainment troupe can take on an aura of glamour; it didn't matter if the costumes were raggedy hand-me-downs and the scenery a piece of cardboard—it was the freedom that attracted young people like Clarence to every shoestring touring company that came to town. Traveling shows represented a means of escape, and Clarence was determined to someday leave Chattanooga with one of them. It happened around 1910 or 1911, and he slipped away without telling his family. "If Bessie had been old enough, she would have gone with him," said Maud Smith, Clarence's widow, in a 1971 interview, "that's why he left without telling her, but Clarence told me she was ready, even then. Of course she was only a child."

Losing the household's oldest male made life even tougher for Viola, who vented her anger and frustration on the rest of the family, which now also included her own baby daughter, Laura. Viola accepted the money Bessie and Andrew generated on the city's sidewalks, but she resented their activity, knowing that it was only a matter of time before Bessie, and possibly Andrew, also abandoned her. "Viola did some terrible things to Bessie," said Maud. "If she did something bad, she'd punish her by keeping her locked up in the outhouse all night." Bessie attended the West Main Street School, going as far as the ninth grade.

One schoolmate described her as "a girl full of mischief"; another recalled that she "pulled all sorts of pranks" if things did not go her way. "Of course, if you weren't bigger than she was, she'd just beat you up, but the other kids used to pick on her so she had to fight back.'

Bessie's opportunity to leave came in 1912, when Clarence returned to Chattanooga with the Moses Stokes company for a limited storefront theater engagement. She was thrilled to see her own brother as the show's master of ceremonies, and one ventures to guess that she was equally impressed by one of the show's female performers, the then-unknown Gertrude Rainey.

Much to Viola's chagrin, Clarence had Bessie audition for the show's managers, who took her on as a dancer. For years, a colorful story that often saw print had Ma Rainey—as she would later be called—play Chattanooga with her own show and literally kidnap young Bessie; one particularly imaginative writer even described a "cursing, outraged" eleven-year-old Bessie being dumped out of a burlap bag at Ma's feet! It has also been suggested that Ma taught Bessie how to sing, but some of her contemporaries remembered otherwise. "[Ma Rainey] may have taught her a few dance steps, or showed her how to walk onstage," said the late stage and film actor Leigh Whipper, who first heard Bessie at Atlanta's "81" Theater a year after she left home, "but Bessie was born with that voice and she had a style of her own when I first heard her in Atlanta. She was just a teenager, and she obviously didn't know she was the artist she was. She didn't know how to dress, she just sang in her street clothes, but she was such a natural that she could wreck anybody's show. She only made ten dollars a week, but people would throw money on the stage, and the stagehands would pick up about three or four dollars for her after every performance, especially when she sang the 'Weary Blues'—that was her big number."

Ma Rainey was the first known female blues singer. She, too, rode to fame in the wake of "Crazy Blues," but she was clearly a pioneer. Her style was not as glossy as that of most emerging blues queens; it was closer to that of the country blues singers, men who roamed the South in the early part of the century. "From the Bottoms of Georgia came the mother of the blues, the Gold Neck Mama of Stageland—Ma Rainey," reads a 1927 Paramount Records publication. "From earliest childhood—Gertrude Rainey felt the blues were expressive of the heart of the south, and the sad hearted people who toiled from sunup to sundown —crooning weird tunes to lighten their labors." Ma Rainey's accompaniments were often by jug bands whose kazoo and washboard sound matched her earthy style, and she was known for wearing glittery headbands and a necklace of shiny twenty-dollar gold pieces. "Bless her heart, she was homely, but people loved her," said Rainey's former pianist, Thomas A. Dorsey, whose gospel songs later laid the foundation for an industry. Dorsey sold soft drinks in the aisles of the "81" Theater when Bessie was a regular performer there. He described her as a "born natural," and does not recall hearing Ma Rainey take any credit for teaching Bessie anything.

We don't know the circumstances under which Bessie left the Stokes troupe, but she was on her own within a year, making the "81" her home base while she toured with such companies as Pete Werley's Florida Blossoms and the Silas Green shows. Shortly after leaving Stokes Bessie worked briefly in the chorus line of one of two companies produced by Irvin C. Miller, who became one of the most powerful black stage producers of the twenties, but Bessie did not fit Miller's mold. "She was a natural singer, even then," he recalled, "but we stressed beauty in the chorus line, and Bessie did not meet my standards as far as looks were concerned. I told the manager to get rid of her, which he did." Miller's "standards" were explained by his slogan: "Glorifying the Brownskin Girl." Bessie was too dark.

During the postwar years Bessie's reputation grew, but without the benefit of mass media it took years of hard work for a performer to gain wide recognition. Thus she was still known only locally in certain areas of the country in 1921, when she moved to Philadelphia. This was the year of "Crazy Blues," but the record people had yet to analyze its success and decide how to cash in on it.

Ma Rainey's Jazz Band,

1925. (From left

to right) Gabriel,

Al Wynn, Dave Nelson,

Rainey, Ed Pollock,

Thomas A. Dorsey.

(facing page)

Over the years, numerous interesting stories about Bessie have circulated—some true, some slightly exaggerated, and others that are pure myth—but no event in Bessie's life has been described by as many disparate accounts as her so-called "discovery."

Frank Walker, the man Columbia Records chose to run its race records division, claimed to have heard Bessie perform in a small Selma, Alabama, dive around 1917. "I don't think there could have been more than fifty people up North who had heard about Bessie Smith when I sent Clarence Williams down South to get her," he said, leaving out the important fact that Bessie had been performing in Philadelphia for some time. "I told Clarence about the Smith girl and said, 'This is what you've got to do. Go down there and find her and bring her back up here.' " Williams didn't have to be told about Bessie, for he had brought her to OKeh's New York studio just two weeks earlier. OKeh rejected her for being "too rough." Piecing it all together, it appears that Williams told Walker about Bessie, having himself heard of her through Charlie Carson, the owner of a Philadelphia race records shop. Clarence Williams probably shopped around to find a record company that would sign a contract with him for Bessie—he found it in Columbia.

Accompanying Bessie to New York for her debut recording session was Jack Gee, a staid, semiliterate Philadelphia night watchman whom she met in 1922 while working at Horan's, a local cabaret. On their first date, Jack—who dreamed of being a policeman—interceded in a robbery attempt, and received a gunshot wound as a result. During the ensuing weeks, Bessie visited him daily at the hospital, and a serious relationship developed. Jack's family was from Virginia, but his mother lived in a Harlem brownstone, which gave Bessie a convenient place in which to rehearse for her recordings. Also living in that house was Jack's niece, Ruby Walker, a teenager with big eyes for show business. "I had never heard of Bessie before Jack brought her to the house," recalled Ruby, who later changed her last name to Smith, "but Jack was all over her, and I knew she had to be somebody to be recording for Columbia." If Ruby needed proof, it was around the corner.

Bessie cut her first sides—"Gulf Coast Blues" and "Down Hearted Blues"—on February 15, 1923, and the coupling sold close to eight hundred thousand copies within the first six months, beating the impressive figures for "Crazy Blues." That must have sent Thomas Edison heading for his Q-Tips; he had flunked Bessie when she auditioned for his own label, entering an "NG"—No Good—next to her name in his studio log.

On the day her first record shipped, June 7, 1923, Bessie and Jack were married at a small ceremony in Philadelphia. There was no honeymoon, for Frank Walker, who now also acted as Bessie's personal manager, immediately sent her on a brief tour to test the waters. Her first stop was Atlanta's "81" Theater, her old stomping ground, but it was hardly necessary to play it safe, for record crowds greeted Bessie everywhere. An account that was carried by most black newspapers was typical:

> STREETS BLOCKED, HUNDREDS AND HUNDREDS AND HUNDREDS WERE UNABLE TO GAIN ENTRANCE TO THIS PERFORMANCE.... BESSIE SMITH WITH IRVIN JOHNS AT THE PIANO BEFORE THEIR OWN SPECIAL DROP OPENED FULL STAGE WITH "NOBODY'S BIZNESS IF I DO," WITH THE "GULF COAST BLUES" FOLLOWING, WHICH RECEIVED HEAVY APPLAUSE, LEAVING THE HOUSE IN A RIOT.

It was only the beginning. The next few years saw Bessie's show grow into a touring company of as many as forty-five people, with its own railroad car and tent. The Bessie Smith show headed south each spring, picked up the railroad car in Atlanta, and toured until Labor Day, when the car was returned to the depot. Then the fall and winter months were spent on the TOBA circuit, a chain of black theaters belonging to the Theater Owners' Booking Association. Entertainers claimed that the initials stood for "Tough On Black Asses," but Bessie's troupe always received special treatment because she was such a draw. Bessie often interrupted a tour to go to New York and make records. Her contracts, renewed annually, required her to make a minimum of twelve sides per year, but she always exceeded that figure. As the mid-twenties approached, the record catalogs were full of blues queens, but none—not even Ma Rainey—could match Bessie's sales.

When he saw how successful she was, Jack quit his job and joined Bessie on the road. At first it was practically a honeymoon, but Jack was a misfit, unable to accept the free-spirited lifestyle that pervaded Bessie's professional milieu. He tried to belong and in so doing began assuming the role of manager, but Bessie left that job to her nephew, T. J. Hill, and to her brother Clarence, who doubled as the show's master of ceremonies and straight man. Clarence's wife Maud said that no one in the show took Jack seriously because he was only interested in the money and in feigning an air of importance: "Jack couldn't even manage himself," she recalled. "He would always have signs saying 'Jack Gee presents Bessie Smith,' and he would call himself a manager, but he couldn't even sell a ticket. He could count money, and he could ask for money, but that's about it."

Mamie Smith's Jazz

Hounds, 1921,

with Bubber Miley,

cornet; Coleman

Hawkins, tenor

saxophone; Bob Fuller,

clarinet; Harvey

Brooks, piano.

Jack's niece, Ruby, was now also with the show, having talked Bessie into hiring her as a chorine. Ruby's main function, however, was that of confidante and running buddy; Bessie needed to have someone close to her when she and Jack were on the outs, and that was happening with increasing frequency. When Bessie realized a dream and brought her sisters to Philadelphia, she stuck a thorn in Jack's side; a mutual hatred had sprung up between him and Viola, who both vied for Bessie's attention, not to mention her generosity. The main problem, however, was Bessie's drinking and debauchery. "We worked so hard," said Ruby, "that we'd meet ourselves coming into the theater. If a show went over big, like Bessie's always did, the manager of the theater would cut it, so, instead of doing three or four shows in a day, we might do ten. Can you blame Bessie for wanting a drink? Having to do all those shows and then also put up with us and our nonsense?" Bessie was now commanding as much as $2,000 a week, but hers was indeed a grueling schedule, and it was beginning to take its toll. As the pressure mounted, Jack became less tolerant and Bessie more defiant. A pattern developed: he periodically left the show to go on hunting trips—or so he claimed—and Bessie used his absence as an excuse for drinking. Eventually, without warning, Jack—a nondrinker—showed up again, the two engaged in a knock-down-drag-out fight, and a period of harmonious

sobriety ensued. "It happened like that all the time," said Ruby. "And when she was sober, no one better mention a party—not until Jack left again. And about his hunting? The only thing my uncle ever hunted had two legs and titties, you can believe that!" In all fairness, it should be pointed out that Bessie was no model of virtue; her sprees usually included liaisons with people of both sexes, and Jack had—on one occasion, at least—caught her in bed with a chorus girl.

In 1927, the blues boom was essentially over and the TOBA experienced its worst box office year. Urban blacks had become more sophisticated and less enthusiastic about an entertainment form that, in essence, was a perpetuation of the old minstrel shows. In rural areas, audiences still laughed at slapstick skits performed in mammy costumes, so tent shows continued to do good business. For a while, Bessie saw no need to change her act; she had always streamlined her big city routines, anyway, and her career showed no signs of slowing down as the decade entered its final year. But 1929 was not going to be a good year for most people.

It was a year when movies began to talk. From the hitherto silent silver screen, Al Jolson exclaimed "You ain't heard nothin' yet!" a pronouncement in which could be read the death of vaudeville, because, with music and dialogue on the screen, theaters would no longer need live shows to lure in the public. As things turned out, talking pictures ended up putting more people in than out of business, and the demise of vaudeville would be the least of Bessie's problems. For her, 1929 began to turn sour in March, when she found out that Jack was having an affair with Gertrude Saunders, one of Irvin C. Miller's most attractive "brownskin beauties." Adding insult to injury, he had put Bessie's money into Hot Mama, a production starring Ms. Saunders. Ruby explained: "Bessie was always giving Jack money or buying him expensive things, trying to get in good with him again, after she had acted so bad and gotten drunk. She gave him a Cadillac, which he gambled away. Well, she was so tired of hearing him talk about how he could produce her show better than anyone, that she gave him the money—I think it was three thousand dollars—and said 'OK, you do the next one.' Poor Bessie, you can imagine how she felt when she found out that he had put half of *her* show money into Gertie's show—that's the only time I ever saw her cry."

Bessie received the news when the show was appearing at Cincinnati's Roosevelt Theater. She barely made it through the show that night, ignored all calls for encores, grabbed Ruby by the arm and hailed a cab. "We went all the way to Columbus where Gertie's show was playing, and both of us were still in our costumes," Ruby recalled. "I don't know what that cab driver thought, but Bessie

Victoria Spivey, 1937.

One of the few women

performers of the time

who's largely self-

written songs were

firmly grounded in the

blues tradition.

knew she'd find Gertie and Jack together." Once in Columbus, they headed straight for the local black theatrical boardinghouse, where Jack and his paramour were registered. Fortunately for her, Ms. Saunders was out, but Bessie confronted Jack and entered the room, slamming the door behind her. "I was scared to death," said Ruby. "I just sat down on the stairs and listened to them go at it. I thought they'd kill each other—they fought like yard dogs." When the door opened, Bessie emerged alone, her face and arms bleeding, her feathers sagging. "People had heard all that noise, but nobody dared go in there, and when Bessie came out, they all just stared and nobody said a word as we walked out to the cab." That night, Bessie walked out of Jack's life.

Less than two months later, Bessie saw a potential career highlight dimmed as she made her Broadway stage debut in *Pansy*, a musical that opened at the Belmont Theater after only two weeks of rehearsals. Bessie's role was limited to three lines and a couple of songs in the final act, but it gave her the opportunity to perform for a white "downtown" audience. It was an offer she should have refused. On opening night, as the audience filed into the theater and the cast waited for the costumes to be delivered, six of the principal players walked out in disgust. A half hour after curtain time, the costumes and six last-minute replacements arrived, but there was little spirit in evidence backstage. Still, Bessie, the show's only real star, stuck it out.

The next day's papers bore devastating reviews. The critics hated the show, but Bessie won them over. Calling *Pansy* the "worst show of all time," and a "new low," the *New York Times*' Brooks Atkinson described vehement hisses and boos, and marveled at the fact that part of the audience stayed for the second act. "Presently the obese and wicked-orbed Bessie Smith was shouting in splitcord tones, that 'If the blues don't get you' neither she nor the devil would know what to do," he wrote. "Since she was the only practiced performer in the company, and a good one, too, the audience thereupon howled 'Bessie Smith' until the poor woman, with a moon-shaped face, was completely exhausted. Three times she came from behind the scenes to break the shock of complete defeat."

Richard Lockridge of the *Sun* called the show "Bad beyond belief," but he also praised Bessie, suggesting that the audience shook the theater with cheers in order to keep her on stage and stave off the other performers. In the *Evening Post*, Wilella Waldorf suggested that Bessie was the real reason anyone bought a ticket for this show. "Miss Smith, a rather weighty personage of great good humor, sang a song called 'If the Blues Don't Get You' over and over and over to wild applause, likewise executing sundry dance steps at intervals by way of variety. Just as it looked as though she might be kept there all night, Miss Smith announced breathlessly that she was tired and that she was too fat for that sort of thing, anyhow, whereupon she was allowed to retire."

Remarkably, *Pansy* lasted for three performances, and Bessie stayed with the show until the end. A month later, she made her only film, a two-reeler with a thin plot built around her singing "St. Louis Blues." Playing a scorned woman who catches her philandering boyfriend with a young lady must have given Bessie a feeling of déjà vu.

Bessie was still recording and maintaining an arduous touring schedule in October, when the stock market crashed. It was not business as usual, however, for both theater attendance and record sales had slipped dramatically. The Wall Street plunge was another nail in the coffin—soon she had to sell her railroad car and cut her touring company down to a handful of members; vaudeville and the TOBA were dying remnants of the past. When she walked out on Jack, he took Ruby with him, and cast her in the Gertrude Saunders show, obviously a move designed to hurt Bessie even further.

As the country suffered the pains of the Great Depression, Bessie's income dwindled. When Columbia dropped her in November of 1931 it came as no surprise; record sales had dropped to such lows that Columbia was itself on the verge of bankruptcy. There were also all-too-regular reports on theater closings, and the Empress of the Blues was forced to suffer such indignities as having Hack Back, "The Ukelele Wonder," accompany her. It was enough to give anyone the blues, but Bessie's luck hadn't completely run out, for she found a cure for her heartbreak: Richard Morgan.

They had met in Morgan's hometown, Birmingham, Alabama, many years earlier, when Bessie was an aspiring star at the Frolic Theater. Morgan was the antithesis of Jack Gee, a dapper fashion plate—with charm to spare—who thrived among people in the entertainment world. Bessie and Richard renewed their friendship in the mid-twenties, when her career was at its peak and he was a popular Chicago party-giver who ran a flourishing bootleg concern under the aegis of Al Capone.

"Richard Morgan used to have this place where he threw big parties, and invited all the big-time entertainers who happened to be in town," recalled Lil Armstrong. "I played there a few times, and so did Louis, and Jelly Roll

Bessie Smith

(facing page)

[Morton], and Bessie Smith—we all performed and everybody let their hair down, it was that kind of place."

"I know from personal experience that my uncle thought Bessie Smith's music was the greatest God had ever put on earth," Lionel Hampton, Morgan's favorite nephew, writes in his autobiography. "Every time Bessie sang, Richard went around shushing people. Nobody was allowed to interrupt her."

Morgan's admiration for Bessie went beyond her music; in the early thirties, their longtime friendship developed into a serious relationship and led to their living together in Philadelphia. With Richard in the house, Bessie didn't have to go far for a drink; Repeal put a serious dent in the bootleg business, but it didn't kill it—there was still a demand for Morgan's specialty: moonshine. "That's all Bessie would drink," Ruby recalled. "She was drinking that bad stuff even when the good stuff was in—she said that anything sealed made her sick."

"They lived in a modest home, and it was comfortable," said publicist Allan McMillan, who visited Bessie and Richard in Philadelphia. "They appeared to lead a happy life—involved with each other, you know—and Richard ran a liquor business out of that home. In fact, I believe Bessie helped him operate it, filling bottles, and so forth, but singing was still her main occupation. She was more marvelous than ever."

In 1933, Bessie again made records: four sides for OKeh, the company that had found her "too rough" ten years earlier. These performances bear out McMillan's assertion; Bessie sounds wonderful singing to "modern" swing accompaniments by a band that included trumpeter Frankie Newton, tenor saxophonist Chu Berry, and—barely audible on one performance—Benny Goodman. It has been said that Bessie's drinking occasionally gave her voice a rough edge during this period, but there is no evidence of decay on these final sides, for which she received a flat fee of $37.50 per selection.

"All singers sound a little rough sometimes, but Bessie was better than all the rest of them, even when she wasn't in good shape," observed Ruby, who was having a hard time working for Gertrude Saunders, and longed to rejoin her aunt. But Bessie no longer had a chorus line; she was working as a solo act again, and not always as the headliner. Life was a far cry from what it had been in the turbulent golden days, yet, with Richard by her side, acting as her manager, Bessie seemed more at peace with herself than Ruby had ever seen her. Long gone was the

income that once allowed her to purchase $5,000 guilt gifts for Jack, but she was still working regularly, and Richard had his own money, saved up from his lucrative Chicago activities.

Bessie's career hit rock-bottom in 1934. She and Richard threw together a touring show called "Hot from Harlem," but it was neither hot nor from Harlem, and audiences stayed away. For the first time, a Bessie Smith show lost money. Toward the end of the year, her appearance at the Harlem Opera House was a disaster. The *New York Age* review was painful:

> BESSIE SMITH IS UNDOUBTEDLY A GOOD BLUES SINGER
> —BUT BLUES SINGERS DON'T SEEM TO RATE AS HIGHLY AS THEY USED TO.
> HER RECEPTION BY THE AUDIENCE, ALTHOUGH WARM ENOUGH, SEEMED TO
> BE ACTUATED BY APPRECIATION OF HER PERSONALITY RATHER THAN HER ACT.
> OF COURSE THE USUAL RISQUE LINES EVOKED THE USUAL OBSCENE HOWLS
> OF LAUGHTER, BUT—SHE WASN'T CALLED BACK AT ALL.

The time for change had obviously come. Bessie had always done well singing nonblues material, especially in the North, but she rarely included decidedly white pop songs, such as the ones favored by New York's sophisticates. When the Apollo Theater on Harlem's 125th Street turned from Yiddish burlesque to black entertainment, Bessie was booked there by Frank Schiffman, who had admired her for many years. She accepted the engagement and decided to use the opportunity to shed the old blues queen image. Dumping the horsehair wigs and headgear, she swept her hair back, smartly, replaced the beaded dresses and feathery fans with elegant satin evening gowns, and presented a program that kissed the Roaring Twenties goodbye.

1936 saw Bessie mingle with stars of the Swing Era. She performed an eleven-week engagement at Connie's Inn, attracting sizeable white audiences from whom she elicited "one of the most enthusiastic demonstrations of approval ever recorded in a night club," according to Allan McMillan's *Amsterdam News* review. It appeared that brighter days lay ahead for Bessie as she elegantly translated her artistry into the new language of swing. "I told everybody in the Goodman band about Bessie being tight with my uncle," said Lionel Hampton, "and Benny said 'Oh, man, we gotta make some records with her.' And I had just signed a contract with Victor Records to do a lot of small-band dates with people like Johnny Hodges, Nat King Cole, and all those guys, so Eli Oberstein of Victor told me, 'Be sure to get Bessie.' "

It was not to be. At around one o'clock on the morning of September 26, 1937, Bessie and Richard Morgan stepped into her old Packard and drove out of Memphis, where she had been appearing with Winsted's *Broadway Rastus* show. With Richard at the wheel, they headed down Route 61, bound for Clarksdale, Mississippi, where they planned to spend the night. It was very dark and the narrow, two-lane highway stretched for miles, straight and mesmerizing. Bessie, her arm resting on the open window, was asleep when the rear end of a large truck suddenly loomed in front of the car. Richard didn't see it until they were almost up under it—then he swerved to avoid a collision, but it was too late. Its red tail lights disappearing into the morning darkness, the truck accelerated and was gone, leaving behind the twisted pile of steel and wood that had been Bessie's Packard. Thrown out of her seat by the impact, she lay unconscious in the middle of the road, bleeding profusely. Unhurt but dazed, Richard staggered and waved his arms frantically at an approaching car.

The other car, a Chevrolet, stopped just short of the wreck, its beams eerily catching the figure of Bessie. The driver was Dr. Hugh Smith, a white intern from Memphis, who—with a friend named Broughton— was heading south on a fishing trip. As Broughton went to a nearby house to call an ambulance, Dr. Smith examined Bessie and concluded that she probably had severe intra-abdominal injuries—in any event, it was clear that her condition was critical. Broughton had just returned when the scenario took a bizarre turn; yet another car, traveling at a fast clip, approached, and the driver showed no signs of slowing down. Dr. Smith jumped on the running board of his own car and started flashing his lights, but the third car just kept coming. "I'll never forget this as long as I live," said Smith in a 1971 interview. "Mr. Broughton was on the right side hollering 'Smith, you'd better jump—he ain't checkin'.' Well, I jumped and Broughton jumped just as this car barreled into the back of my car at about 50 miles per hour. It drove my car straight into the wrecked Bessie Smith car and made a real pretzel out of it—it was a total loss. He ricocheted off the rear of my car and went into the ditch to the right. He barely missed Mr. Broughton and Bessie Smith."

Clarksdale had two hospitals, one for blacks and one for whites. It turned out that the truck driver had also called an ambulance, but he—not having seen Bessie and Richard—phoned the white hospital, so two ambulances showed up, one from each hospital. The black ambulance took Bessie, but it was already too late. She died at 11:30 that morning, without ever regaining consciousness.

The New Masses Presents

AN EVENING OF AMERICAN NEGRO MUSIC

"From Spirituals to Swing"

DEDICATED TO BESSIE SMITH

CONCEIVED AND PRODUCED BY
John Hammond

DIRECTED BY
Charles Friedman

American Negro music as it was invented, developed, sung, played and heard by the Negro himself—the true, untainted folk song, spirituals, work songs, songs of protest, chain gang songs, Holy Roller chants, shouts, blues, minstrel music, honky-tonk piano, early jazz and finally, the contemporary swing of Count Basie, presented by the greatest living artists from the South, the Southwest, and Negro communities in the North. The first comprehensive concert of the true and exciting music of the Negro. With pianists Meade Lux Lewis, Albert Ammons, Pete Johnson, James P. Johnson; blues singers Ruby Smith, Robert Johnson; Mitchell's Christian Singers; finest Negro dancers

Count Basie
AND HIS ORCHESTRA

Willie Bryant, Master of Ceremonies

FRIDAY EVENING, DECEMBER 23, 1938

Carnegie Hall

SEVENTH AVENUE AND 57th STREET, NEW YORK CITY

News of Bessie's death was widely reported and there was no talk of racism in connection with the accident until the following month, when a *Down Beat* article played up a bit of hearsay that Bessie died because she was refused admittance to a white hospital in Memphis. Despite glaring inconsistencies, the rumors became the accepted account of Bessie Smith's death, and no one paid attention when a 1941 inquiry by John Lomax produced letters belying them.

"The car in which she was riding was smashed and she was in shock when brought to the hospital," wrote Dr. W. H. Brandon, a doctor at Clarksdale's Afro-American Hospital, in 1941. "She died some eight or ten hours after admission to the hospital. We gave her every medical attention, but we were never able to rally her from the shock…. you may brand the statement that she was refused treatment as an absolute untruth."

It is said that Richard Morgan never was the same after the accident. "I saw him a couple of years later," said Ruby, "and I hardly recognized him."

"Richard never forgave himself for Bessie's death," writes Lionel Hampton in his autobiography. "He kept saying he should have avoided that truck. He couldn't even say Bessie's name without crying. He was never the same after that. He got real old real fast, and he died just a few years later. I believe that he grieved himself to death over Bessie."

Bessie Smith was buried in Philadelphia, her grave remaining unmarked until 1970, when rock singer Janis Joplin and a Philadelphia nursing home owner split the cost of a stone. The inscription came from Columbia Records' publicity department: "The Greatest Blues Singer in the World Will Never Stop Singing."

ROBERT JOHNSON

TOWARDS A ROBERT LEROY JOHNSON MEMORIAL MUSEUM

by Al Young

The famous photograph is the first thing to catch my eye as I step inside my much-imagined Robert Leroy Johnson Memorial Museum in Greenwood, Mississippi. At a Saturday night dance in Three Forks, fifteen miles from Greenwood, in the summer of 1938, Robert Johnson, so stories go, got very sick after he drank from an unsealed half-pint of strychnine-laced whiskey the vengeful owner of a popular Delta juke joint had presumably earmarked for him. Johnson, a professional entertainer, obsessed with music, women, and wanderlust, had evidently been seeing the roadhouse owner's wife on the sly. But this particular weekend, Johnson—along with bluesmen Honeyboy Edwards and Sonny Boy Williamson II (Rice Miller)—had been performing at the juke at the owner's invitation. When Johnson became so ill that he could no longer play or sing, he was driven back to Greenwood, where he died that Tuesday, August 16.

To look at this nice-looking, smallboned man beaming so openly, warmly tinged with shyness, resplendent in his steam-pressed, pinstripe

suit, I can only guess that there must've been a slew of women, married and unmarried, who wouldn't have minded taking their chances with such a visiting musician.

The picture is actually one of two shots Robert Johnson posed for in Memphis, when his nephew was leaving town to hitch up with the navy. They say that the companion picture shows Uncle Robert and the teenager posed side by side, but few have ever seen it. And, frankly, who needs it? What mere picture could ever be big enough to contain a world-sized fellow like Johnson? Or even match the aural snapshots, sketches, and portraits he left us of himself.

Standing there at the entrance, overjoyed, I still can't believe that some semitangible form of tribute is finally being paid to this legendary blues genius, whose influence, more than fifty years after his death, continues to color and fuel the blues, as well as its off-color offspring, rock and roll.

While I'm suspended in that state, animated by imagination, wondering where I can get me a suit as sharp as Johnson's, a little brownskinned gent in short sleeves and tie—the museum guide, I gather—sort of floats up to me. There's something special, almost spectral about him. Clearly accustomed to dealing with reverential Johnsonites, he takes good care not to pop my dream bubble.

"Ain't no fixed donation," he tells me in resonant Southern tones, "but we do appreciate whatever you can contribute."

"Oh, sure," I say and reach for my wallet. At the same time, I can't help staring at this wiry fellow. In white shirt and glasses, with the belt and suspenders he wears to keep up his well-worn but pressed seersucker britches, he makes me think of those straight-backed, hat-wearing Baptist men I grew up around; men who might raise natural hell on a Saturday night, then turn around and preach blood-boiling fire-and-brimstone sermons in their Sunday-go-to-meeting gear.

Of course it isn't everyday I get to hang out in such illustrious history. Even rarer is to run into another black person—African-American, if you will—concerned about blues preservation. After all, whenever I turn up at a blues festival in the U.S.—unless popular blues-and-soul artists are headlined: B. B. King, Koko Taylor, Bobby Blue Bland, Katie Webster, Etta James, Albert Collins, James Cotton, or Robert Cray—I can count on being just one of handfuls of nonwhites peppering the crowd. And don't let any of the old authentic or even halfway authentic country blues survivors take to the stage at a so-called blues festival today. An air of amused bewilderment, which is actually a kind of courteous resentment, will often fall over the audience.

"If you have any questions, feel free to ask 'em," the friendly man says, then takes the bill I hand him and tucks it into the slot of a collection box.

"Sir, is there a guidebook? Do you have a scheduled tour?"

"Why, yes—" He hands me a modestly printed booklet with the identical dapper Johnson on its cover. Eyeing it again, I think automatically of blues great Johnny Shines, who traveled extensively with Johnson between 1935 and 1937, throughout the South and on up into Chicago, Detroit, and Canada. It was Shines who said: "Robert could ride highways and things like that all day long and you'd look down at yourself and you'd be as filthy as a pig and Robert'd be clean—how, I don't know."

"That'll be two dollars, please, " the museum keeper says. "Far as tours go, I just now got through showing a group of people from overseas around this place. Europeans mostly, but it was some Japanese mixed in with 'em." He gives his watch a worried look. "Fact of business, I was thinking 'bout going on my break. But maybe I could be inspired to walk you through the museum and give you a little rundown—if you got the time. We got a few pictures and a mural the Arts Council got some local artists and college kids to do. We even got a little listening room, where you can kick back and enjoy a taste of that good music of Robert's."

Even as I wonder how much "inspiration" a tour might end up costing me, I can't help liking the old guy.

Finally he holds out his hand and says, "I'm Luther Washington."

"Oh, " I say, closing in for the handshake, "Al Young."

"You from round here?"

"Not really," I explain. "But I *was* born in Mississippi, the year after Johnson died."

"Where bout?"

"Ocean Springs—over there on the coast near Biloxi."

"Hmmph," he snorts and clucks his tongue knowingly. "That's Walter Anderson country. He was *some* painter, wasn't he?"

"Yeah," I say, "Anderson's art rules on the coast, but the Delta here is Robert Johnson country."

From the way he looks me up and down, I can tell Mr. Washington is as curious about me as I am about him. Taking an educated stab at what I might be up to, he says, "You some kinda critic or scholar or something?"

"No, Mr. Washington. I'm just a poet—and a Robert Johnson fan of course."

"Is that a fact?" Luther Washington looks tickled. "Well, even though I am older than you, don't be scared to call me Luther. A poet, hunh? Now, to me, that's what Robert was—a poet."

Luther's words land bull's-eye smack in my heart. Way back when the sound of him first blew into my life, it was the poetry Robert Johnson stirred up, while he was dusting his musical broom, that had swept me off my feet.

It was in 1961, and Columbia had just brought out the first of its two *Robert Johnson, King of the Delta Blues Singers* albums. These, of course, were sides Johnson had cut in November of 1936 at San Antonio, Texas, and in June of 1937 at Dallas for the American Record Company's Vocalion label. Everything connected with those recordings is now gilded with myth. H. C. Speir, the white music shop owner in Jackson, who auditioned and made records of area talent in the back of his shop; the man Johnson came to see about getting himself recorded. Ernie Oertle, the regional scout for ARC, who got Johnson's name from Speir, and was impressed enough when he heard Johnson to bring him over to San Antonio, where A & R man Don Law and recording director Art Satherly recorded him at the Gunter Hotel. In three working days Johnson cut sixteen sides.

It is from Law that we get the famous stories about how Johnson, asked to play for a group of Mexican musicians that ARC was also recording, absolutely refused to play while facing them. "Johnson turned his back to the wall," Law said. "Eventually he calmed down sufficiently to play, but he never faced his audience." And there is the companion story Law told of having to go Johnson's bail after he got himself locked up for vagrancy. Fearful of having the recording schedule blown, Law virtually locked Johnson up in a San Antonio hotel. Within hours, Law got a telephone call from Johnson. "I'm lonesome," Johnson told him. "You're lonesome?" Law asked. "What do you mean, you're lonesome?" Then Johnson is reported to have said: "I'm lonesome and there's a lady here. She wants fifty cents and I lacks a nickel."

Historic sessions they have indeed, become. At the time, however, Johnson, like many a gifted dark horse musician, was being groomed strictly for the so-called race market; that is, for black record buyers. His "Terraplane Blues," which is still being analyzed, deconstructed, and ooh'ed and ahh'ed over by blues cognoscenti, was actually a late thirties hit.

By the time Johnson went back to Texas—this time to Dallas—six months later, he was something of a star.

By 1961 I was singing and playing folk music in coffee houses and cabarets, and keeping company with so-called folkies, who relished being hip about the legends surrounding black country blues artists. But what blew me away about Johnson weren't apocryphal myths but, rather, haunting, raw, beautiful music he made; it was Johnson's heart-stopping guitar work and that plangent, soul-priming catch in his voice; his cry.

To me, that cry told the whole history of human longing and hurt; it told Johnson's personal story, too. The cry in Robert Johnson's music is the same one that always makes me heat up and shiver when I listen to great ethnic music. That cry, seemingly a kind of longing or yearning, is firmly fixed all over the globe in soulful musical idiom. Whether it be African-derived devotional music, gypsy flamenco or *cante jondo*, traditional Balkan and Slavic song, karnatic music of Southern India, Gregorian chant, Scots-Irish balladry, Japanese koto song, Indonesian, Hawaiian, or Middle Eastern music, or African song in its complex varieties—this cry sweetens and deepens them all.

Urgency is what I've always heard in Robert Johnson's cry. Totally devoted to music, as we now have learned, Johnson appears to be proof that latter-day anthropologists, in defining the human species, are wise to cite religiousness

as one of our intrinsic attributes. Whether it be God or some manner of divine intelligence, nature, mankind, love, wealth, fame, glory, or power in any of its infinite forms, including sheer sensual pleasure, we seem to have an indwelling need to believe in something grander or, in any case, bigger than ourselves, to which we're willing to sacrifice the little self; something immeasurable by which we might measure ourselves and the meaning of being alive. As mythologists such as the late Joseph Campbell elaborately point out, it is as though we are forever questing for something we need to complete ourselves; something that promises to dissolve the painful notion that we are born on earth to suffer time and loss, then die. Can there be any form of human expression more worldly than the blues? And yet Robert Johnson, the greatest of Delta blues artists, in his beautifully sad "Stones in My Passway," could cry to us:

> *I have a bird to whistle and I have a bird to sing;*
> *Have a bird to whistle and I have a bird to sing;*
> *I got a woman that I'm lovin', boy, but she don't mean a thing*

For Johnson, that something seems to have been music, even though his obsession with women and with unrequited love might have run music a close second. The sonic urgency so evident in most of Johnson's recordings has about it an unutterable quality that is not unlike what speakers of Spanish call *duende*. In its goblinesque, demon-like aspect, as well as its aspect of charm or personal magnetism, the power of *duende* is spiritual.

Even today, decades after I first heard Johnson sing, "You better come on/in my kitchen, baby/it's goin' to be rainin' outdoors," I still think I know the exact kitchen he might've had up his sleeve. It was my grandmother's kitchen, with no electricity, no running water, in the town of Pachuta in Southeast Mississippi's Clarke County, all farm and piney woods back then. The sound of Johnson's quivering voice was as ancient as rain to my ear; it whetted my poetry-starved appetite.

I could smell the dusty, sweet, rain-damp earth, barnyards, hickory nut shells, and big-leafed fig trees waving in the high, cooling breeze that always rose before a storm. And I could feel the warmth of the woodstove, even taste the leftover cornbread and turnip greens and scraps of blackeyed peas, the purple remains of blackberry cobbler; see and smell dishwater souring in a deep, round, enamel pan, and squint at the table draped with fading, checkered oilcloth. And the whole wicked while, the wick of a kerosene lamp would be burning down slow; a dry, heated, sniffable flame at the dark-dead end of day.

When Robert Johnson cried, "I got to keep movin'/I've got to keep movin'/blues fallin' down like hail/blues fallin' down like hail…And the days keeps on worryin' me/there's a hellhound on my trail/hellhound on my trail," I had no trouble picturing either the hellhound or the trail.

I could see the man slipping through the woods by stark moonlight, out there past the spring, where Mama used to send me and other grandkids with capped glass jars and jugs to collect stream-fresh mineral water. And the hellhound? He would be night-black; wild, feral, and funky, huge and scraggly-looking, with red-hot fireplace coals for eyes, and yellowed-out, scissor-sharp teeth.

But what was Johnson running from? Where did he think he was headed? I sometimes wondered this in the space of the same few moments I might've taken time out to wonder about the lifetime flight of jazz ace Charlie "Bird" Parker (Johnson's junior by only eight years) or the poet Dylan Thomas's hellish inclinations. The generation of black entertainers born around the turn of the century up through the twenties, not all that long after Emancipation; so many of those great blues and jazz performers—and there were con artists and hustlers among them—led self-destructive lives.

While Ferdinand "Jelly Roll" Morton, for example, early jazz's premiere pianist and composer, might not qualify temporally, it can't be altogether dismissed that his original intention was to use his fabulous musical talents as a front for his pool shark ambitions. A legend in his own mind, Morton, the self-proclaimed inventor of jazz, figured that if he played things right, he'd be headed for bluer skies than he'd known in New Orleans, and greener pockets, too.

Robert Johnson was headed, like me, or so I imagined then, in my lavishly romantic adolescence, straight into the heart of darkness. After all, that was the surest way to reach the light, wasn't it?

Over the last half century, Robert Johnson—who seems to have absorbed more blues influences than any other blues artist—has had a greater impact on the blues and, by extension, American popular music, than any other single musician. His impassioned singing and astonishing guitar techniques—which go together like bees and flowers—have had a powerful influence on musicians the world over, from Jimi Hendrix, Ike Turner, Robert Lowry (who could win any Robert Johnson sound-alike contest), Taj Mahal, and Robert Cray, all the way back to Elmore James, Muddy Waters, Howlin' Wolf, Robert Nighthawk, Eddie Taylor, Johnny Shines, and Baby Boy Warren, to name a handful. This isn't to even begin to speak of Johnson's influential white, rock-embedded exponents like Eric Clapton, John Paul Hammond, Johnny Winter, Keith Richards, and Bonnie Raitt.

It was Robert Johnson who brought to blues guitar-playing the so-called turnaround chord which ended on a dominant seventh instead of the tonic. And it was Johnson's refinement of his hero Charlie Patton's boogie-woogie walking bass line that paved the way for the electrified Chicago blues, and the rhythm and blues of the forties and fifties, which had a pronounced effect on late-century rock and roll. But mainly Robert Johnson brought to blues performance a personal commitment and emotional intensity at a level so high that artists working in the idiom today may still measure themselves or be measured by standards he set in the thirties.

So affecting was the sense of passionate intensity Johnson's bottleneck slide guitar and voice-cry emitted that one of his prime disciples, Muddy Waters (born McKinley Morganfield) is sometimes credited, rather simplistically, with having brought the electric guitar into blues-playing, thereby preserving the passion and intensity of Delta blues while updating them for up-north, urban ears. Waters, who loved Johnson's music and regarded Johnson as his main influence, put the Mississippi Delta's Stovall plantation behind him—geographically, at least—when he moved to Chicago in 1943. A year later he bought his first electric guitar, mostly to make sure what he played would be heard when he worked Southside Chicago bars with a band that eventually included Jimmy Rogers, Little Walter Jacobs, and "Baby Face" Leroy Foster. But, as Robert Palmer points out in his lovingly penned *Deep Blues: A Musical and Cultural History of the Mississippi Delta*:

"Muddy and his associates can't claim to have invented electric blues, but they were the first important electric band, the first to use amplification to make their ensemble music rawer, more ferocious, more physical, instead of simply making it a little louder. And they spearheaded the transformation of Delta blues from a regional folk music into a truly popular music that developed first a large black following, then a European following, and finally a worldwide following of immense proportions."

Big Joe Williams,

a typical Mississippi

blues musician.

Williams was most

closely associated with

the song, "Baby

Please Don't Go."

(facing page)

The proportions of any one musician's influence on music can never be satisfactorily calculated. It is safe to say, however, that Johnson not only set standards; he wrote a few, too: "Sweet Home Chicago," "Dust My Broom," "Rambling on My Mind," and "Love in Vain" have all become classics, recorded and rerecorded by scores of blues, folk, pop, and rock artists—from Elmore James and His Broomdusters, Robert Jr. Lockwood (Johnson's stepson), and Otis Spann to Ike and Tina Turner, Taj Mahal, and the Rolling Stones.

Stories stack up in the blues history books about Johnson, who played harmonica well as a boy; stories about how hopeless he sounded when he first took up guitar, which he loved. According to ear- and eyewitness accounts, Johnson's technical and emotional proficiency on guitar took a not-so-quiet quantum leap forward during his late teen years.

It wouldn't be until late 1963 that I'd meet Bukka White, the guitarist, pianist, and harmonica player, who was splitting the bill with me at the Jabberwock, a relatively elegant restaurant and cabaret on Berkeley's Telegraph Avenue. Folk music was in and so were old-time, rediscovered blues musicians. Gifted guitarist John Fahey and his buddy Ed Denson had unearthed Bukka White at a Memphis rooming house, and brought him out to the San Francisco Bay Area. During that period, White and I were also turning up on the bill, separately, at the Cabale, a funky, ultrabohemian Berkeley folk club down on San Pablo Avenue. It still thrills and intrigues me to ponder what I remember White saying about Robert Johnson, although, as I've come to realize, it was doubtless more hearsay than daresay; their paths as performers don't seem to have ever crossed.

"Robert couldn't play," I remember White saying. "He was pitiful. He'd slip out the house and try to play with Son House and them, but he wouldn't be doing nothing. Then, a year and a half slip by, and here he jump up sounding like y'all heard him on that record. Now, you mean to tell me he ain't made some kinda deal with the Devil?"

The early sixties was the folk blues revival era. Enthusiastic and enterprising young Yankees were systematically journeying South, sojourning, and returning with valuable cargo—Furry Lewis, Mississippi John Hurt, Mississippi Fred McDowell, Sleepy John Estes, Hammie Nixon, Bukka White. It was possible to drop by Jon Lundberg's Guitar Shop on Berkeley's Shattuck Avenue of a slow afternoon, and shake glad hands with Texas songster Mance Lipscomb, a marvelous discovery of Berkeley-based Arhoolie Records's Chris Strachwitz.

One night, in the Cabale dressing room, Lipscomb told me: "Frank Sinatra is all right with me. He's putting my new record out [Lipscomb had just signed with Sinatra's newly-formed Reprise label], and give me enough money to get me a new pickup truck to ride my dogs around in back. Yeah, I'm doing all right." Oldtimers like Lipscomb, White, Lightin' Hopkins, and Big Joe Williams—

and numerous others I'd heard and learned about from relatively obscure sources—were being resurrected and booked into folk clubs, college concerts, and festivals throughout the U.S., the U.K., and Western Europe. The revival biz was whizzing right along by 1963.

Two years later, 1965, in the pages of the folk music magazine *Sing Out*, Son House, companion to Willie Brown and perhaps one of Johnson's most important teachers, told folklorist Julius Lester: "Willie and I were playing again out at a little place east of Robinsonville called Banks, Mississippi. We were playing there one Saturday night, and all of a sudden somebody came in through the door. Who but him! He had a guitar swinging on his back. I said, 'Bill!' He said, 'Huh?' I said, 'Look who's coming in the door.' He looked at me and said, 'Yeah, Little Robert.' I said, 'And he's got a guitar.' And Willie and I laughed about it. Robert finally wiggled through the crowd and got to where we were. He spoke, and I said, 'Well, boy, you still got a guitar, huh? What do you do with that thing? You can't do nothing with it.' He said, 'Well, I'll tell you what.' I said, 'What?' He said, 'Let me have your seat a minute.' So I said, 'All right, and you better do something with it, too,' and I winked my eye at Willie. So he sat down there and finally got started. And man! He was so good! When he finished, all our mouths were standing open. I said, 'Well, ain't that fast! He's gone now!' "

The dramatic possibility/idea that Johnson actually might have sold his soul to get so good at singing and playing blues guitar in such a short spell has been shoveled up and heaped so high and deep around the Johnson legend that it continues to fertilize world imagination. Who doesn't love a good story? As often happens, myth and hearsay are so firmly rooted in the planting of the Johnson legend that it has become difficult to tell the true flower from its hothouse look-alike.

The 1986 movie *Crossroads*, directed by Walter Hill, gave us a thoroughly Hollywoodized account of how this sort of devil's deal is cut. In the film, a young, contemporary Long Island white classical guitarist and Juilliard student named Eugene Martone (played by Ralph Macchio) takes a janitorial job in a nursing home in order to get next to a man he believes to be Willie Brown, Johnson's fabled early mentor and sidekick. At a dusty crossroads, shot in sepia-tone to dramatize Brown's disturbing flashback-memories of himself, we see Brown as a young man literally signing a written contract with Legba, a Southern U.S. version of the West African trickster-deity. In exchange for his soul, Legba will make Willie Brown a blues ace. Later, at another crossroads, shot in full color to represent more or less contemporary Mississippi, it's an aged Devil-as-trickster we meet. He snidely proposes a way for Willie Brown and Eugene "Lightnin' " Martone to "buy back" Willie's soul. For collateral—after Martone tells this folksy devil, "I don't believe in any of this shit anyway!"—the Devil wants nothing less than this simpering white boy's soul.

People all down the ages have never tired of stories thick with the Faust motif, in which someone makes a no-win pact with the Devil by exchanging or sacrificing priceless spiritual treasure for worldly wealth, knowledge, or power. And since instruments of Satan will always have strings attached, banjo-players, guitarists, and fiddlers often play the central role in this ageless myth.

Like Niccolo Paganini, the great violinist and composer, Johnson was at times known to conceal his chords and fingerings from other musicians when he performed in public. What better way to either arouse or confirm public suspicion and rumor? Both geniuses were believed to have struck bargains with the Devil. The truth, though, is that Paganini's father drove his prodigy son mercilessly in his violin studies, so that by the time Paganini was thirteen, he was known as the "wonder child." And, like Robert Johnson, who openly encouraged rumors of his satanic bedazzlement, Paganini—whose cadaverous appearance enhanced his own sinister image—seems to have known quite well that such a reputation, if work were playing theater and concert gigs, sold tickets.

Was Robert Johnson himself selling wolf tickets? Considering the frequency with which he made musical reference to either Hell or the Devil, expressed his impending sense of personal damnation or infernal doom—and given Johnson's admiration for players like Peetie Wheatstraw, who bragged of being hell-connected—it wouldn't be hard to build a case for Johnson being a sly, far-seeing self-publicist, who knew the value of a canny showbiz gimmick. Wherever he went, especially after his Vocalion singles came out, he never failed to draw crowds.

While developing his own electrifying playing and singing styles, Johnson borrowed licks, motifs, colorations and rhythms, specific phrases, lyrics, and whole songs from numerous predecessors as well as from pop blues artists of his era, the twenties and thirties. His long-awaited recorded legacy of some forty-one known recorded sides, alternate takes included, was not made available until half a century after his death.

Blind Willie McTell

represents the apogee

of the Atlanta, Georgia,

twelve string guitar

tradition. McTell was

to Georgia blues what

Johnson was to the

Mississippi Delta blues.

(facing page)

Being a lot more interested in music than school or sharecropping, Johnson took up the Jew's harp, then the mouth harp (or harmonica) before settling down with guitar in his late teens. It isn't difficult to see how anyone with any semblance of ambition would've schemed to break away from the various plantations where he grew up and, for the most part, lived his brief life.

From his earliest days—at a time when his mother was partnerless, an itinerant Delta labor camp and plantation worker, doing the best she could to provide and care for her daughters Bessie and Carrie and baby son Robert—Johnson had seen and known hard work. Once his mother found and married Dusty Willis, they raised Johnson to the brink of adulthood on the Abbay and Leatherman plantation in Robinsonville. Because of Johnson's contempt for picking cotton and any other kind of field labor, he and his hardworking stepfather didn't get along.

When Johnson first got married, he and his bride took up residence with his older half-sister Bessie, and her husband on the Klein plantation near Robinsonville in Copiah County. Music must have been a powerfully attractive alternative to hard labor for someone like Johnson, who learned to play harmonica, tap-dance, sing, and play guitar. By the time he and bluesman Johnny Shines met up in 1935 and hit the road together—sometimes hoboing and hopping freights with Shines's guitar-picking cousin Calvin Frazier, who had killed a man— the charismatic Johnson, always musically astute, had become quite the versatile crowd-pleaser.

"Robert could play anything," the eloquent Johnny Shines in interview told equally eloquent American music portraitist Peter Guralnick. "He could play in the style of Lonnie Johnson, Blind Blake, Blind Boy Fuller, Blind Willie McTell, all those guys. And the country singer—Jimmie Rodgers—me and Robert used to play a hell of a lot of his tunes, man. Ragtime, pop tunes, waltz numbers, polkas —shoot, a polka hound, man. Robert just picked up songs out of the air. You could have the radio on, and he'd be talking to you and you'd have no idea that he'd be thinking about it because he'd go right on talking, but later he'd play that song note for note. Hillbilly, blues, and all the rest."

And there are stories about Johnson, just before his death, playing electric guitar in a drummer-backed band that sounds as if it might have been influenced by swing jazz and the just-emerging black urban style, grounded in shuffle rhythm and boogie accents, that came to be known as jump

music. According to Stephen C. LaVere, the photographic archivist and Robert Johnson historian, "[Johnson] took St. Louis, Detroit and New York in easy stride. His musical approach was altered a bit—he began playing with a small combo. He used a pianist and a drummer in a Belzoni jook joint—the drummer had 'Robert Johnson' painted in black letters across his bass drum—before a large crowd of people, a good many of them musicians. And as he was able to play anything people wanted, he began to concentrate less and less on the blues. He may have gotten away from it almost entirely had it not been for some divine intervention."

LaVere, who holds copyrights to at least two existing photographs of Johnson (the famous Memphis studio shot of him all suited up; and another, taken in a dimestore booth, that shows him in shirtsleeves, suspendered, all sullen and sad-eyed, with guitar in tow and an unlit cigarette dangling from the left side of his lower lip) is one of three men who have devoted much of their lives to filling in the glittering, titillating holes and gaps that made Robert Johnson's life so enticing to admirers and musicologists. The others are blues sleuth Gayle Dean Wardlow, the first to track down Johnson's death certificate, and Houston folklorist Mack McCormick, whose *Biography of a Phantom*, snatches and fragments of which have turned up in journals and blues tracts over the years, is surely the most famous unpublished manuscript about the lubricious Johnson. The book shows every sign of being definitive.

If you discount the first things his older half-brother Charles Leroy (their mother loved the name Leroy) showed him on guitar, or the later, inescapable influence of Robinsonville's "Whiskey Red" Brown and Myles Robson, Johnson's earliest in-the-flesh musical influences were Willie Brown, another town resident, who sometimes worked local juke joints with the roving, rambunctious Charlie Patton, who, even then, was a legend: an extraordinary, smoke-and-whiskey-throated, white-looking blues veteran.

Plantation parties, barbecues (also known as get-backs), levee camps, logging camps, and juke joints; fish fries, country dances, sandlot ball games, road houses—these were some of the lucrative venues accessible to the likes of these blues songsters throughout Mississippi between 1916 and 1934.

Aside from his living models, there were country and urban blues artists and stylists whose recordings fascinated Robert Johnson, and from whom he borrowed during those formative years. They include pianist Leroy Carr and guitarist Scrapper Blackwell (their 1928 "How Long Blues" was one of

Johnson' s earliest "learning" tunes, and Blackwell's 1928 "Milk Cow Blues" begot Johnson's "Milkcow's Calf Blues"); singer and instrumentalist Lonnie Johnson (whose vibratoless, matter-of-fact vocalizing Robert Johnson imitates coolly on "Drunken Hearted Man" and "Malted Milk"); slide guitarist Kokomo Arnold (his "Sagefield Woman Blues" and "Old Original Kokomo Blues," a 1934 race record smash, directly and respectively inspired Johnson's best-known classics, "Dust My Broom" and "Sweet Home Chicago"); the professional bootlegger William Bunch, who sang under the name Peetie Wheatstraw, billing himself variously as the High Sheriff from Hell or the Devil's Son-in-Law, and whose sexual savvy—so his macho, braggadocio lyrics let on—was a direct result of his close "family" connections; Skip James, whose 1931 Paramount recording of the sadistic, even mean-spirited "22-20" became, in Johnson's deft hands, the "32-20 Blues" (James's "Devil Got My Woman" probably inspired Johnson's "Hellhound on My Trail"); and the Mississippi Sheiks (Johnson closely followed their bestselling "Sitting on Top of the World" to create his ruefully erotic "Come on in My Kitchen").

There were records by others (Henry Thomas, Johnnie Temple, and Casey Bill Weldon, for example) that Johnson assimilated as well. *The Roots of Robert Johnson*, a valuable anthology released in 1988 by Yazoo Records, features tracks by several of these persuasive country blues stylists.

Robert Johnson's biggest singing inspiration, however, was Eddie "Son" House, a preacher and bluesman who served a year in Mississippi's infamous yet fabled correction facility, Parchman State Farm, but set up residence in Johnson's home base of Robinsonville. In House's emotional vocalizing, secular and sacred seem to fuse in a fury of locked horns and ruffled wings. Listening to him and to the Robert Johnson his vocal spirit begot, it's possible to experience almost directly the two-faced, flipsided fervor of the blues and gospel idioms. Saturday night the term of endearment is Baby; Sunday it's Jesus—and both call for great rejoicing. One listen to Son House's "My Black Mama, Pt. l" or "Preachin' the Blues, Pt. l" is enough to convey the raw, emotionally uninsulated, high-voltage vocalizing of House's vocal style. So urgently dramatic it must have set the intense, teenage Johnson's soul on fire when he first heard it.

To arrive at his "Walkin' Blues," Johnson slowed and steadied the tempo of "My Black Mama," shaped it into a twelve-bar blues, and allowed his guitar to "talk back" exquisitely to his lyrics, which contain one of the loveliest poetic descriptions of feminine physical magnetism in all of recorded blues:

She got, uh, Elgin movement from her head down to her toes
Break in on a dollar most anywhere goes. Ooo oooooooooo
To her head down to her toes (Oh, honey,
Lord) She break in on a dollar most anywhere she goes

Like practically everything else about him except his music, the details of Robert Johnson's childhood are as sketchy as any blues lyric; nothing about the man is easy to pin down, much less fill out.

He seems to have been born May 8, 1911, at Hazlehurst, Mississippi, to Julia Dodds and Noah Johnson. Robert's mother, however, wasn't legally married to Robert's father but, rather, to one Charles Dodds, an independent farmer and furniture maker. In 1907, under a cloud, and in the face of a lynch mob, Dodds had been forced to abandon Hazlehurst for Memphis, where he was going by the name of Spencer.

Although she had to accept the fact that besides their daughters Bessie and Carrie, Dodds-Spencer also had children by a live-in mistress, Julia was briefly reunited with Charles Spencer in his Memphis household. With her she had brought little Robert—the "outside" child whom Spencer resented—and Carrie, Robert's baby half-sister. But before long she'd moved back to Mississippi, without her children, to the cotton-farming town of Robinsonville. There she married Willie "Dusty" Willis, an exemplary, no-nonsense, dust-raising farm laborer, who didn't cotton much to the kind of foolishness music represented. Dusty Willis became Robert's new stepfather from the age of nine, when he was sent from the Spencer home in Memphis back to the Delta to live with Willis and Robert's mother. Robinsonville remained Johnson's home base until he was grown, at which time he seems to have beat a path back to Hazlehurst, his birthplace, to find Noah Johnson, his biological father.

Before leaving the Robinsonville area altogether, Johnson —who by then must have been somewhat "mannish" (i.e., sexually precocious) fell in love with fifteen-year-old Virginia Travis, whom he married early in 1929 at Penton, Mississippi. The two moved in with Johnson's half-sister Bessie, officially

Mrs. Granville Hines. That summer, during their stay with the Hineses on the Klein plantation near Robinsonville, Virginia got pregnant. Neither the baby nor Virginia, however, survived childbirth.

While you'd certainly have to had been in Robert Johnson's shoes to know exactly what he felt, it's still possible to imagine his desolation. "Crossroads Blues" could very well have described his feelings in the wake of that grave personal tragedy. So awesome is the sense of loss and the feeling of abject, prostrate desperation projected by Johnson's breaking voice and guitar in this key recording that it continues to give fiery credence to the notion, which Johnson the performer helped promote, that he had come by his musical powers occultly.

> *I went to the crossroad, fell down on my knees:*
> *I went to the crossroad, fell down on my knees;*
> *Asked the Lord above. "Have mercy now, save poor Bob, if you*
> *please"...*
> *I went to the crossroad, mama, I looked east and west;*
> *I went to the crossroad, baby, I looked east and west:*
> *Lord, I didn't have no sweet woman, ooh, well, babe, in my*
> *distress...*

Never much for either school or sharecropping, and now armed with a guitar, Robert Johnson started hitting the roadhouses and other gigs with Willie Brown and Son House. Under the sleepy-looking but watchful and teacherly eye of the older, Alabama-born blues guitarist Ike Zinnerman, Johnson would soon be working around the timber mills, the road gangs, and, of course, the ever-jumping jukes.

Two years later Robert Johnson married again, this time to Calletta "Callie" Craft, who, by all accounts, adored and served him faithfully. In the mounted photo enlargement of her that hangs in my mind-erected Robert Leroy Johnson Memorial Museum, Callie Craft, all got up in in what was probably her Sunday best—white dress, white stockings, white cloche, and black pumps—looks a little vulnerable, yet strong and long-suffering; not quite like someone who enjoyed dancing or sitting on her husband's knee while he performed.

Was this originally a secret wedding picture to go with her secret marriage to Robert? Who snapped it? Finally it's the serious, "I'm-for-real" aspect of her; the overeasy melancholy that makes her eyelids droop, the bittersweet radiance of her face, so vulnerable that I can't help wondering if it was the worshipful Calletta (whom he abandoned to devote the rest of his life to playing music and serious rambling) on that quiet, reflective cut he called "When You Got a Good Friend":

> *Wonder could I dare apologize*
> *or would she sympathize with me*
> *Mmmmmm mmm mmm*
> *would she sympathize with me*
> *She's a brownskin woman*
> *just as sweet as a girlfriend can be ...*

Irresistible, too, is the temptation to speculate further about Johnson's abandonment of Callie. Did it flavor the sentiments expressed in his devastating "Kindhearted Woman Blues"?:

> *I got a kindhearted mama,*
> *do anything in this world for me*
> *I got a kindhearted mama*
> *do anything in this world for me*
> *But these evil-hearted women,*
> *man, they will not let me be ...*
> *She's a kindhearted woman she studies evil all the time*
> *She's a kindhearted woman she studies evil all the time*
> *You well's to kill me as to have it on your mind ...*

Given all the women Johnson mentions by name in his music, it would be practically impossible to guess which fictitious or real-life lovers might have inspired which of his songs. In his ground-breaking work, *The Bluesmen: The Story and the Music of the Men Who Made the Blues*, Samuel Charters takes a sloweddown look at Johnson's sweethearts and many flames.

"Many blues men spent a lot of time thinking about women," Charters writes, "but Son House remembers that Robert was driven by sexuality. The relationships at least left Robert with names to use in his songs. His 'girl friends'—the term he used in 'When You Got a Good Friend'—included Beatrice in 'Phonograph Blues,' Bernice in 'Walking Blues,' Thelma in 'I Believe I'll Dust My Broom,' Ida Bell in 'Last Fair Deal Gone Down,' Betty Mae in 'Honeymoon Blues,' and Willie Mae in 'Love in Vain.' There is no way of knowing who they were, or if they were anything more to him than someone to spend a few nights with in a new town."

That Robert Johnson, in fashioning his thrilling song repertoire, seized upon and synthesized whatever he heard, saw, experienced, and felt is now as clear to me as the sound of that famous octave-slide with which he introduces "I Believe I'll Dust My Broom." What hasn't been so clear—and why should it?—is what went on in that same restless mind to turn Johnson into an absolutely obsessive rambler and rake.

While notions about what psychiatric therapists might have to say about Johnson's behavior roll around in my head (*He was looking for love and acceptance. He was away from his mother for too long and felt rejected, then his father rejected him, too—and so did his stepfathers! His first wife and baby died on him. There was no strong sense of family. He came from a twice-broken home. He was the outside child. His childhood was far too peripatetic to produce a healthy, stable adult*), my ears pop open to what Luther Washington, the museum guide, is telling me that odd, factually-researched-but-situationally-hazy afternoon.

"The way it came down to me," Luther says, pausing to make sure he's got my attention, "is that Robert used to go looking for women he figured would be glad to even have him look at 'em. They wouldn't necessarily be the prettiest women, but they would be the kind that'd be flattered to be all up, under and around somebody like Robert—a sharp-dressing musician, kinda delicate and good-looking. Well, from what they say, Callie Craft was like that. She taken good care of Robert. Like the song say, she picked the seeds outta his watermelon and put a pillow up under his head; kept him well fed and dressed and didn't ask him where he was going or when was he coming back. Now, you just didn't hardly run up on that type of woman everyday, you know.

"So Robert," Luther continues, "he laid around Hazlehurst a coupla years, learnt everything he could from Ike Zinnerman, and practiced every minute he could. They say a lotta the East Coast sounding blues that Robert put out might've come from Zinnerman. Ain't no way of telling, since Ike never made a record. What's amazing to me is all the stuff Robert picked up off records. He was the first one to come along, far as blues is concerned, and put all them country styles together, then turned around and put 'em in a trick."

"How do you mean," I ask Luther, "'put 'em in a trick'?"

"Well," says Luther, "Robert Johnson put some type of spin on everything he shot for. After he got through popping 'em one, they not only stayed popped; they was headed someplace else, too. And he knew what he was doing, too. Didn't matter to him where he himself or anything else was headed, long as it was moving."

"Luther, I've always been crazy about the way Johnson closed 'Dust My Broom.'"

"Sing it for me," says Luther.

I'mo call up China,
          see is my good girl over there:
I'm gon call up China,
          see is my good girl over there,
If I can't find her on Philippine's Island,
          she must be in Ethiopia somewhere.

"You got a nice voice," Luther tells me. "But what is it fascinates you about those words?"

"Luther, how could someone who threw around global references like that actually believe Chicago was in California?"

"Hard to say. But he sure as hell knew it wasn't down here in Mississippi, didn't he? One of the things we'd love to get our hands on for our collection is the little book Robert used to write his songs down in. Wouldn't that be something to have around here! I understand he had pretty handwriting, too."

"Now, how would you know something like that?"

"His old running buddy Johnny Shines put that out. Aw, it's so much we'll never know about Robert Johnson, don't care how many bits and fragments they try to glue together."

"How long did he stay with Callie?" I ask Luther.

"Evidently not all that long. He walked out on her and their kids and left Copiah County for the Delta. Then he went back to Robinsonville; that's where he blew Son House and Willie Brown's minds with his singing and picking. He hit the Delta part of Arkansas—Helena and West Helena—and that's

where it all started coming together. Robert started playing with everybody that came through there—and going off everyplace. Helena was a jumping little river town, wide-open; that's where Robert Johnson came to be Robert Jr. Lockwood's stepdaddy, I reckon you might say. Robert taken a liking to the boy's mother and moved in with her. Her name was Estella Coleman, but she answered to Stella. And, I'll tell you, Robert must've been a good teacher, too; that Robert Jr. Lockwood can go!"

"He sure can!"

"Can't he play the blues? Down here in Mississippi, we're just starting to appreciate a lot of the old blues and the people who played 'em. You might say that culture—blues and storytelling, literature—is one of our heaviest exports. We had to fight Greenville to get this little museum put up here in Greenwood, and it isn't all that much, but it's a beginning."

Already, way down the hall in the next room, I can see a portion of the mural Luther mentioned when I first walked in, and all I can make out are some Mexican-looking fellows in big sombreros, the kind worn by mariachi musicians. I can hardly wait to see what the mural is all about.

"Look here," says Luther, "I'm not trying to make out it's things I know about Robert Johnson that don't nobody else know. I got most of my information from the same sources you probably got yours—from other people's writings and interviews and all like that. But I am old enough to remember when records like 'Terraplane' first came out."

"Really? What was that like?"

"Well, I had to listen to it on the sly, you know. But I liked it. My daddy caught me at it one time, though. You know how it is being a preacher's kid; feel like you got to prove to everybody that you regular and OK. My folks didn't much allow me to be listening to no blues, not up in the house anyway. My daddy was a preacher and my mama taught school. They were kinda on the sanctified side. The blues represented everything they were trying to forget. But, I got to admit, I loved 'Terraplane Blues,' and I know it had something to do with my daddy owning one."

"But I thought you said your parents didn't approve of blues records."

Luther laughs. "Naw, I'm talking about the car, not the song! The Terraplane was a six-cylinder sedan that Hudson Motors put out. And sometime they'd let me drive it." A devilish gleam lights up Luther's eyes as he sings a verse of Johnson's "Terraplane Blues" lyric out loud:

Now, you know the coils ain't even buzzin',
      little generator won't get the spark;
Motor's in a bad condition,
      you gotta have these batteries charged.
But I'm cryin' pleeease,
      pleee-hease don't do me wrong;
Who been drivin' my Terraplane now for
      you-hooo since I been gone? ...

"What you think?" Luther asks, turning to me. "Think I coulda made a living singing the blues?"

"You might have to get a little help down at the crossroads," I say.

"Aww, man, don't come bring that up! I'm so tired of this crossroads stuff I don't know what to do. All the people they talked with—friends, his women, all kinds of people—and they all say Robert played that guitar all the time; I mean, *all the time*. One woman I read about said she got up in the middle of the night one time and seen him standing by the window in the moonlight fingerin' his guitar. Anybody with that kinda obsession is bound to get good in a hurry, don't you think?"

"But the crossroads myth *sounds* so good."

"Yeah, I know," says Luther as I follow him into the mural-walled room. "But, see, we have always had these hoodoo and conjure people all 'round down in here. It's plenty Negroes my age from the South know about John the Conquerer root, root doctors, silver dimes, rabbit and coon feet, mixing up hair with nails and needles and thimbles, mojo hands, goofer dust, and all such as that. And you better believe Robert knew it, too. But that don't mean he had to be on good personal terms with the Devil to play as outstanding as he did."

Luther looks around, as though to make sure we're still the only ones in the museum.

"Tell you," he says in a low voice, "sometime it's weeks'll go by before anybody colored walks through that door. Plenty of white folks show up, though, especially white folks from overseas. And lately it's been a lotta Japanese, too. You know, the Japanese be all down here in the Delta nowdays, with all kinds of business development projects and what-have-you. You can stand right there at the airport in Greenville and watch 'em fly in and out. They probably know more about the blues than I do, all I did was live 'em."

"Luther," I say. "The other day I was listening to Robert Cray...."

"Sure," Luther interrupts, "I know him ... young fellow, used to play with Albert Collins, put out that *Strong Persuader* album."

"Yeah, well, Cray was being interviewed on the radio, on Terry Gross's show, 'Fresh Air.' And he was saying that you don't find too many black people at blues festivals or patronizing the blues because the blues mostly represents things we'd just as soon forget."

"Sure, like bad luck and hard times and all like that. My folks thought like that. My daddy caught me listening to a Robert Johnson record one time and he took the record off the victrola and broke it. Said, 'You listen at this, then next thing you know, you'll be drinking and gambling and laying around with these old donies'—that's the name they use to have for lowlife women—'and hanging around places where you get your head cut. After you leave my house, you can listen at whatever you want to. But as long as you under my roof, there won't be any blues.' "

"Do you think your father was right?"

With an undecipherable grin twitching around his lips, Luther looks at me and looks at me for the longest. Then he breaks out into a dark little laugh and says, "Yeah, I would have to say yes, Reverend Washington knew what he was talking about. But there's another side of the blues that sanctified people like my folks didn't realize."

"Which is..."

"You know how Robert Johnson sings, 'She's a kindhearted woman; she studies evil all the time'? Well, the Bible does say: All things worketh for good. It's a lotta holier-than-thou types that's got evil minds. By the same token, I know a gang of blues singers that spend a lotta their time thinking about God and trying to straighten up. The way I see it, you go far enough in any one direction, you gonna come out the other side, and meet yourself going the other way. Now, let's go in here and look at this mural and listen to us some Robert Johnson."

"You're right," I tell Luther, reaching to shake his hand again. "If I'm feeling bad and listen to some good blues, sometimes it makes me feel better just knowing others suffer, too."

When I extend my hand to touch Luther's, he suddenly breaks into song. Suddenly I'm shivering, my arm breaking out in goosebumps. That's when it hits me how much he sounds like Johnson—*exactly* like Robert Johnson— and he's playing the sultry afternoon air like a guitar that sounds like Johnson's, too. It's quite as though Luther Washington—if there ever was a Luther Washington in the first place—is lip-synching or miming Johnson's electrifying record of "Preaching Blues (Up Jumped the Devil)":

> *The bluu-uuu-uues*
> *   is a lowdown shakin' chill;*
> *Mmmmmm-mmmmm ...*
> *   is a lowdown shakin' chill;*
> *You ain't never had 'em, I*
> *   hope you never will.*

When I blink hard and look again, there is no Luther. There's no Robert Leroy Johnson Museum; only the sound of this century's pioneer modern blues genius, crying in what I now think actually might have been the Greenwood, Mississippi, night. The only thing I'm certain of is that the music is as real as it is haunting.

T-BONE WALKER

ELECTRIFYING TEXAS BLUES: AARON "T-BONE" WALKER

by Helen & Stanley Dance

Rain, rivers and floods—in the South often the cause of widespread distress—were once recurring motifs in the blues. Bessie Smith's harrowing "Back Water Blues" was one of her greatest records, and T-Bone Walker was undoubtedly familiar with it when, accompanied by a piano player, he made his first record in Dallas a couple of years later. It was called "Trinity River Blues," and the fact that the Trinity River is still a mean old river was shown once more in 1990 as it devastated large areas of the Texas countryside.

T-Bone was nineteen years old, already well acquainted with the blues tradition, as one of those young men who had taken Blind Lemon Jefferson, his guitar and tin cup along Dallas's bustling Central Avenue. Jefferson, a highly influential blues singer, was one of the essential sources of the younger man's music, but in the decade before T-Bone recorded again there were to be profound changes.

José Antonio
·HOLLYWOOD·

The vaudeville dominance of such women as Ma Rainey, Bessie Smith, Clara Smith, and Ida Cox won them in later years the honorific adjective of "classic," but even in their prime there were strong male challengers. And by the end of the thirties, these women had been eclipsed by male singers.

T-Bone Walker was certainly familiar with the traditions of both male and female blues artists. Besides his experience with Blind Lemon, he had heard a good deal of one of the most advanced blues guitarists of the day, Lonnie Johnson. He had played in several Texas dance bands and also worked with Ma Rainey and Ida Cox before moving to California in 1934. The major influence in his singing, however, was the immensely popular Leroy Carr, a pianist who had recorded over 150 titles before his death in 1935, many of them with a formidable guitarist named Scrapper Blackwell.

Leroy Carr

(facing page)

Descriptive labels for blues, such as rural, country, and urban, are convenient to use but hard at times to define. The wholesale migration of blacks from the rural South to the industrial North caused many changes. Compared to the country singers, Leroy Carr was more sophisticated, clearly of the city; but despite his smoother style he delivered the blues with a telling conviction that registered strongly with black record buyers. The urbanization of the blues, in fact, proceeded rapidly during the thirties as the influence of jazz, with its then-current emphasis on swinging, made itself increasingly felt. What was known as the "Bluebird beat," for example, was largely developed in Chicago by the talented stable of bluesmen who recorded for that label, but it had its counterparts on the company's chief competitors, Vocalion and Decca.

The blues beat had generally become more compelling by the time T-Bone made his second appearance on records in 1940, this time with a jazz orchestra led by Les Hite and containing such notable players as Britt Woodman, Walter Williams, and Al Morgan. Because Hite's musicians did not like the sound of amplified guitar in the rhythm section, Walker mostly played the acoustic instrument. His experience in bands, however, had much to do with the intense swing he brought to blues playing. Even more important, however, was the extraordinary fact that both he and Charlie Christian had been tutored by the same man—Chuck Richardson—in Oklahoma City. Both recognized the potential in the electric guitar, and while Christian went on to become the paramount influence on jazz guitar, T-Bone became the greatest influence on blues guitar. Eddie Durham, the arranger and trombonist, was sometimes thought to have pioneered on the electric instrument, but he readily gave credit:

"T-Bone was the first I heard playing it, though I'd been fooling with it, too. But 'Bone was as big in blues as Charlie was in jazz, the greatest I ever heard."

T-Bone always claimed he had been born with the blues in his soul. Part of his unerring rhythmic gift clearly came from his earlier experiences as a dancer. (He and Christian, in fact, had worked out dance routines *together* as young men.) Then, too, he was born with a voice and an ear, so that by the time he had paid his early dues he was ready to introduce something fresh with a virtually new technique. B. B. King, who became a lifelong admirer and credited him with being the prime cause of his own desire to play the blues, always stressed the importance of T-Bone's touch and sound, "the prettiest sound I think I ever heard in all my life." The sound, perhaps, had something to do with the way T-Bone held the guitar, not parallel to his body, but turned at an angle perpendicular to it. This sound could be both incisive and delicate, and it was served by a superb sense of dynamics, which gave it a very personal, dramatic quality. The intensity of his rhythmic punctuations was varied to great effect, and the character of his melodic line could range quickly from nostalgic and biting single-note lines to chords powerfully exultant. Moreover, he seemed wholly at ease at any tempo, from slow to what in jazz is termed "up," and he had an almost infallible gift for choosing tempos perfectly appropriate to the content of his lyrics. He was also much responsible for the popular "Texas guitar shuffle"; his own "T-Bone Shuffle" became a standard against which all others were measured.

As a singer, Walker proved largely inimitable. His phrasing was subtle and sensitive, his voice light and expressive, and his singing perfectly attuned to the flights and accentuations of his guitar playing. Emotionally, these elements were of a piece, so that his performances were equally convincing on the many different levels the blues attains.

He was famous for his showmanship, which he had developed before black audiences in Texas long before entertaining became a malpractice. He would play the guitar behind his head and he might end a brisk number by doing the splits on the dance floor, all the time maintaining his own high musical standards.

In short, his was a style of more variety, more swing, and more imagination than had previously been heard on blues guitar. Its immense influence was profoundly felt on a long line of blues guitarists. Besides B. B. King, Clarence "Gatemouth" Brown, Albert Collins, Freddy King, Pee Wee Crayton, Pete "Guitar" Lewis, and Shuggie Otis are among those who have reflected it most creditably.

More than a link between country and urban blues—or between the blues of the twenties and those of the forties (and beyond)—T-Bone's music linked the disparate worlds of jazz and blues. His role was unique and of all his talented contemporaries he was the only one to qualify in both.

"No need of him working out in fields all his life,"
Movelia announced to her husband, Rance Walker, when their son, christened Aaron
Thibeaux and born in 1910, was barely a year old. Aaron's maternal grandfather
cut and stacked lumber in northeast Texas where mills had sprung up alongside the
KATY track. Edward Jamison and his wife Martha, a fullblooded Cherokee, were
strict church-going people and Movelia, a teenager in a family of fourteen, chafed
under their rule. In Rance, whose people were sharecroppers in nearby Conroe,
Movelia had envisaged escape but she came to realize country ways resolutely battled
change. So, looking for the kind of life she wanted for her baby, she set off for
Dallas where her sister-in-law lived.

"Mama and I remained very close," T-Bone said. "And
you wouldn't believe how good she could strum, before ever she married my Dad.
When Blind Lemon Jefferson or Huddie Ledbetter came by Dallas, she'd fall right in
with them and they'd be singing the blues so great. I'd lay in my little bed listening,
staying awake half the night."

His mother often sent him into town with Blind Lemon.
After they would get set on a street corner, crowds would gather and, taking Lemon's
tin cup, T-Bone would shake it and pass it around. Other times he'd kneel in the dirt
under the windows of the Holiness Church, his heart pounding as he listened to the
preacher call on the Lord. "My pulse would be racin' when the hand-clapping got
going real good," T-Bone recalled.

When he was ten years old, because he then had a
stepfather who played string instruments of every kind, he was allowed to go out in
the neighborhood with a family band that featured mandolins, guitars, and violins.
When a crowd collected, his uncles would wind up the show by having him dance
and then pass the hat. He was as eager to dance as to sing and he was always
learning new steps. Like Louis Armstrong, he was a natural showman, completely
at home on stage.

When T-Bone was twelve years old, his mother had
bought him a banjo; he had an instrument of his own at last. But this did not satisfy
him for long. He was determined to buy a guitar, and this he accomplished during
his junior year at high school by playing weekends at church socials.

When he had got into high school he had joined Lawson
Brooks's band, which played the Tip Top Cafe on Central Avenue every weekend.

"We had sixteen pieces," he remembered, "and I had to use a banjo to be heard. Some of the guys, like T. W. Pratt and Mike Lacy, could arrange, and in time we got up enough nerve to try some of Duke Ellington's stuff."

But T-Bone ended up thinking that since there was always work to be had, he preferred to be on his own. Charlie Christian took his place with Brooks, and later Buddy Tate joined the band as well. "I was sorry to leave," T-Bone said, "but by then Mama was alone like before. Again it was only her and me, and I didn't want to go out on the road." Before he had left grade school he had gone off one summer with Dr. Breeding's medicine show. And once, while still a freshman, he had run away to hook up with Ida Cox's troupe of singers and dancers, then touring the state. But eventually the sheriff got to him and made him turn around and go home.

When Cab Calloway played the Dallas's Majestic Theater in 1929, T-Bone got the break he had been hoping for. He was the winner in an amateur show at that time and the prize was a week's work with Calloway's band. In Houston Cab let Walker have a solo spot with an act he'd worked up playing banjo as he went down in the splits. Later that year a Columbia records talent scout approached him about a record date. As Oak Cliff T-Bone (a name related to the area of Dallas he inhabited) he recorded two originals on guitar, "Wichita Falls" and "Trinity River Blues," both sites with which he was familiar.

Before the end of the year Count Biloxi, a white Russian who was fronting a band out of Hollywood with which he toured the Southwest, hired him as part of a Ted Lewis–type of act. "I was his shadow, I guess," T-Bone recalled; "while I played guitar, and danced, I was also mimicking him. They mostly played top spots and the pay was good. But one thing bothered me. I was the only colored guy in the band. So, because of the girl singer, there were places where things got stormy. Like at Blossom Heath in Oklahoma City, some roughnecks came backstage and a couple of the guys and myself had to take to the fire escape."

Young enough to be foolhardy, T-Bone, who was expected to lie low for a day or two, instead lit out for Kansas City. Not only had he never been there before, but he landed with people who set out to take advantage of him. Drinking had become such an early habit that while still a teen he had acquired stomach ulcers from which he suffered for the rest of his life.

"I had to borrow where I worked to get train fare to bring him home," his mother said. "He was a mess. We carried him to the hospital right away.

"That was the first time," T-Bone remembered, "but it wasn't the last. Over the years I have been bedded in any city you care to name."

But in 1934 he had no knowledge of the headaches that were to come. He was enjoying every day, and every minute of the day. At the Gem Hotel in Fort Worth, he was fronting a quartet, playing guitar, singing, and doing time-steps. There he met Vida Lee, his wife to be. Improbably, this was his first serious romance, and despite all odds it lasted a lifetime. But it brought to an end the halcyon days of extreme youth. T-Bone began to think of L.A. Though he and Vi lived with his Mum, there was never enough cash, so to get ahead he would have to leave town.

He located a company that was ferrying automobiles to the West Coast. "They were looking for drivers, and they took me on. You never got paid, but you got a free ride. We each drove a car and towed one in back. I had a dollar in my pocket when I landed in L.A. But I met a guy who said he'd take me around and that night we headed for Little Harlem. You had mud streets in Watts back then, and the Brown Sisters' place was out in a field." Big Jim Wynn, the baritone saxophonist, who, with his band, accompanied T-Bone on the road in later years, had formed a group which featured Zutty Singleton on drums. "He said he didn't need a showman, because Zutty was a show in himself. But I was allowed to dance ... and I had me a job. I ended up singing, playing guitar and emceeing, as well."

"Things were always jumping," Phace Roberts, the dancer, remembered. "Weekends you had a time getting near. By then 'Bone was singing, and chicks would get excited, cross the floor, climb the bandstand and hand him money. They snapped fingers as they strutted on back to their seats. People went wild. We never let him quit 'til the wee, wee hours."

Zutty swore that when T-Bone came up from the splits, hitting the strings way up in the air, each time he got through there'd be fifty dollars more in the kitty. With people lining up to pay out the cash. The cash enabled T-Bone to join gamblers who frequented the dressing room. The stakes were not small, sometimes four and five hundred dollars, but when luck was with him, T-Bone liked to party and everyone would be invited. Eddie Durham often brought the Sweethearts of Rhythm by after hours and T-Bone asserted, "I never play-acted when they were out front, because those chicks really swung."

Over the next three years, in and out of clubs like the Alabam and the Plantation, T-Bone's popularity continued to grow. 1940 saw a change when Marili Morden, one of the founders of the Jazz Man Record Shop (she later married Atlantic Records's Nesuhi Ertegun), thought it was time for T-Bone to break out of Watts. She took him to MCA and had him booked into the Trocadero on the Strip. "Present him in tails, " she said, "like any big-time act." She followed up with Billy Berg's place on Vine Street and when T-Bone told her his regular fans were being excluded from the club, she persuaded the management to introduce a new policy which welcomed all comers. This was a first for the West Side but paid off handsomely. Soon after, T-Bone was hired as a featured singer by Les Hite and his band, who were stationed at the Sebastian's Cotton Club but scheduled to make a tour that would take them to the East Coast.

By now T-Bone and Vi had been apart for four years. "Long as you keep gambling," Vi had told him, "no sense my coming to L.A." But this was different, T-Bone felt, and he persuaded her to join him on the road. Continuously practicing backstage, by the time they reached New York he had effectively mastered the electric guitar although Elite continued to feature him exclusively as a vocalist, even on the recording the band made for Varsity.

Returning to Los Angeles, T-Bone opened once more at the Alabam and there Joe Louis and Charlie Glenn, joint operators of Chicago's Rhumboogie Club, caught his act. "Here is the entertainer to star in our upcoming show," Louis said. Hoping to rival the Grand Terrace with a Cotton Club formula, they were prepared to spend money on a lavish show. T-Bone had entered on a new phase in his career. Backed by Milt Larkin's territory band out of Texas, in settings devised by producer Ziggy Joe Johnson and featuring Marl Young's arrangements, success was assured and Chicago accorded T-Bone a royal welcome. He saw his name in lights for the first time and during the next two years he was brought back over and again to star in new productions. In 1945 on the Rhumboogie label, accompanied by local musicians rendering Young's at times inappropriate arrangements, he recorded early versions of his best known hits.

His return to Los Angeles later that year heralded a marvelous epoch, a critical period in his career. He signed a contract with Comet Records which allowed him to record on the Black and White label and hire the best musicians in town. "I was lucky," T-Bone said, "because Ralph Bass, who was an exceptional A and R man, supervised our sessions." Dating from the days when he had recorded Dizzy Gillespie, Dexter Gordon, and Wardell Gray, Bass had considered himself a jazz fanatic and was a great T-Bone fan. From mid-1946 to the end of 1947, fifty titles were recorded featuring an outstanding group of Los Angeles musicians.

The trumpet players were variously George Orendorff, Teddy Buckner, Jack Trainor, and Al Killian; the tenor saxophonists Jack McVea and the incomparable Bumps Myers; and on piano T-Bone used the idiosyncratic, inimitable Willard McDaniel and the blues specialist Lloyd Glenn. Oscar Lee Bradley from Les Hite's band was on drums, and Billy Hadnott or Arthur Edwards played bass. Subsequently these Black and Whites established T-Bone's reputation as the father of the electric blues. His hits were acclaimed as they appeared and were featured coast to coast on Top Ten radio programs.

T-Bone Walker,

London, 1968

(facing page)

The bluesman Lowell Fulson remembers that from that time on T-Bone was a sure-fire success on the road. He was often booked in a triple-threat blues package which might feature Ray Charles, Wynonie Harris, Jimmy Witherspoon, Joe Turner, or Fulson himself. "We'd take to arguing," the latter recalled, "about who would close the show. It might be Big Joe who would say: 'I'm going to. You know who I am,' and someone else would counter, 'I'm so and so, I am the one!' So then I'd volunteer to open, and we'd have to let T-Bone close because no one could follow his act!"

While he was on tour he learned Vi was pregnant. After eleven years of marriage a baby was on the way. He hurried home, ecstatic; later at the hospital the nurses said, "He was going to whip us, because we wouldn't let him take over."

"Before Bernita was a year old," Vi recalled, "he had her on the road with him. When they were taking a plane, he slung her over his shoulder while his valet carried their bags. When he went to work and everyone was hollering, 'We want T-Bone!' he would appear with that baby riding on his hip!"

When Harold Oxley, who had managed the Jimmie Lunceford band, signed T-Bone on, he arranged to send him out with a band that belonged to and was fronted by baritone saxophonist Jim Wynn.

"Oxley was experienced, and T-Bone was crazy about him," Wynn remembered. "He booked us in spots where the jumps were okay and the money was right. We used practically nothing but heads [i.e., informal arrangements] and it got going so good, it was soon obvious we were a big attraction. T-Bone's hits kept us up there and this went on for two or three years. The crowds got bigger, and the money increased. Everything was laid on just right. The only drag was when T-Bone had to cancel a date.

"He was supposed to drink nothing but milk, goat's milk at that! He claimed he could spot a goat a half mile away. Trouble was that after the gig T-Bone would get to playing cards with locals who were waiting on him. He'd stay up half the night and feel bad the next day. Suddenly the pain would be worse, and Oxley would be down and spirit him away. That happened two or three times, like where he'd stay in the hospital a week. Any other office would have dropped us long ago, once we'd been sued. Still it continued like that till Oxley died, which was the blow that did us in."

Afterward T-Bone had to quit the road altogether and face up to an operation which had been put off too long. "Them doctors," he said, "good as robbed me of my stomach. I came round all right, but had to let the band go."

Later, with his nephew, who was billed as T-Bone, Jr., he headlined variety shows in night spots and vacation hotels. "Things hadn't exactly slowed at that time," he said, "because Muddy and Hooker were doing okay, but word got around that my condition was poor. People said it was heart."

In 1960, however, the breaks came his way again. Count Basie hired him to appear with his band in a big package show that featured stars George Shearing and Ruth Brown. "I'd have paid my own salary just to hear those Basie cats blow," T-Bone said, "but somehow I thought I didn't fit the slot that Jimmy Rushing and Joe Williams had occupied. Basie treated me great and said not to do anything rash because the band was going to Europe the following year. But I cut out, just the same. I didn't feel right."

Still, in 1962 he got his chance with a package called Rhythm and Blues U.S.A. Booked by German concert promoters Lippman and Rau, the unit featured what T-Bone called "a bunch of friends": Memphis Slim, Shakey Jake, Willie Dixon, John Lee Hooker, Helen Humes, Jump Jackson, Sonny Terry, and Brownie McGhee. They played concerts in France, Italy, Germany, Denmark, Sweden, Switzerland, and England, and in Hamburg they made a record titled the "American Blues Festival" which featured T-Bone on piano and delighted his fans.

In the late fifties, due to persistent poor health, he had recorded less and less. Where formerly he had one or two albums released every year, it was now some time since anyone had approached him about making anything new. That, however, was to change. He became a great favorite in Europe, where he recorded a number of times for Jean-Marie Monestier's Black and Blue label, and in 1968 he opened in Paris at Les Trois Mailletz where he alternated with Memphis Slim. There he picked up the tabs that all his friends and musicians ran up. He was drinking a bottle of gin a day and another at night and the problem was to feed him. During the many years he had suffered from gastric ulcers, his drinking had been contained but now, without pain after the operation and away from home, he found Parisian nightlife impossible to resist. Always a big spender and ill-advised in the company he kept, when Polydor records expressed interest in recording him he took on new management and no longer bothered about his business affairs at all.

By an odd twist of fate, on returning to Los Angeles in 1972 he discovered that a Grammy had been awarded the album he had made. This boosted his confidence in the new management team. He was now fronting a group of New England youngsters interested in the trendy music that was fashionable at that time. They were unrelated to the type of musician he had worked with all his life. But because he never failed the music, although seldom sober, he attracted younger players and they responded to him. He found himself booked into night spots and theaters where, puzzled, he faced audiences unconvinced about what they heard and unsure of how to respond to it. Nevertheless, the bookings continued and since he never troubled himself about travel arrangements or hotels, he was satisfied.

His family, nevertheless, had been concerned for some time and Vi had tried to persuade him to rest. But during a layoff in L.A., as he and Eddie Vinson set out to play a Central Avenue gig, T-Bone, momentarily distracted, rammed into a car which had stopped for a light. On this occasion he landed in hospital for several months and his injuries confirmed more trouble with his chest. Never patient, he couldn't wait to get out. The Allman Brothers, very big at the time, had recorded his "Stormy Monday" and it was being aired by deejays from coast to coast. T-Bone was in a hurry to get to his publisher right away.

"Stormy Monday" had been a money-maker throughout his career, and maybe now it would take care of him for the rest of his life. Take care of the family too. Now the hospital insisted that he had to check in every three months. Something was wrong, even he had to admit. But he'd see about that number, his number, which would give him time to recoup.

It wasn't to be. The windfall, while he was laid up, had mysteriously disappeared. His group had disbanded, and the bookings dried up.

Some months later, he went out for the last time, and I (Helen) went along. The show was in Pittsburgh at the Nixon theater where he'd played before. Hooker was the headliner, John Lee, whom he'd introduced to listeners many years ago. "My guys will back you," Hooker told him. "Don't worry at all." "Use a chair," we said, "like John Lee does." "No way," T-Bone replied. "Never have, never will." I had to leave him in Pittsburgh, to return to New York. I asked Vi to call me the minute she got him back. Two days went by before I heard. "He stopped off in Houston," she said. "Been having a ball with his friends."

When he returned home he seemed for a time to be himself again, but on New Year's Eve he suffered a stroke and entered a nursing home. He was a cat with nine lives, his friends maintained, but in the spring it was clear he was slipping away. He died on March 15, 1975, and a thousand fans, hoping for a last glimpse of him, jammed the streets leading to the Angelus funeral home.

T-Bone Walker

(facing page)

BIG JOE TURNER

THE HOLLER OF A MOUNTAIN JACK

by Murray Kempton & Arthur Kempton

It seems to me that when I was young my father made a gift to me of Bessie Smith, Billie Holiday, Joe Turner, and Lester Young. Bessie Smith exposed me first to the inside feelings of girls I would begin to know in high school, girls who drank Tiger Rose and ginger ale, liked to do the boogaloo, decided to love somebody when they wanted for as long as they wanted and held families together for as long as they could when their times came to do it. From Lady I would learn about what girls I knew in college thought being in love was supposed to be like for women who were tragic. I had been to Rome as a child, stayed long enough to look around, but from Lester Young I learned to call elegance by its name. He was my professor of aesthetics. Joe Turner was left behind as surrogate for the man who in a time now long since gone, when circles were unbroken, would have been around to teach the boy what he could about being a man. About how to carry himself in life. Joe Turner sang to men about being a man, cynical, romantic, tender, menacing, marginal…

"It was early one Monday morning and I was on my way to school…" I can remember being thirteen years old and writing his lyrics on the covers of my school books. "That was the morning that I broke my mother's rule…"

When I broke my mother's rules, the soundtrack of my memories of the perfumed flesh I pressed in corners at parties, illuminated dimly by naked red bulbs, was written by Curtis Mayfield and Smokey Bill; and then James Brown began blacktopping the road that even now leads no further than to where he brought it. I would still invite Mr. Turner back once or twice a year, like a visiting elder, to remind me that Negroes I knew who thought they were new were no newer than he was when he was the new Negro, who didn't humble up, who went where he pleased, and was bold to say that it's your time now but it's gonna be mine some day.

A.K.

The whole of Bessie Smith's run was over in less than fifteen years, but Joe Turner roamed through five decades of being discovered, being half-forgotten, and then being rediscovered again and again. He broke as a revelation upon the young in the thirties, and then submerged into their never-to-be-as-susceptible-to-stirrings middle age, and then rose up once more as a revelation to the young of the fifties. He had made himself proprietor and distributor of the nursery songs of two generations of adolescents.

He first surprised me into joy in 1939 when my own adolescence had grown stale from lasting too long and when we knew the music far too well and were at risk of that most dispiriting of slides, the one that descends from enthusiasm to pedantry. Our tastes were languishing toward the antiquarian. Jelly Roll's New Orleans, Bessie's Clarksdale, and the Chicago of Tesch and Muggsy were getting to be our home; and then Bill Basie announced and Joe Turner proclaimed that we weren't compelled to stay.

"Roll 'Em Pete" and "Cherry Red" crashed upon our archaeological digs with the clangor of the recognition that the blues were not artifacts but the music's essence and that he who proceeded from this knowledge could say in beseechment or in defiance just what he wanted to. He could tell us that men could be hard and that men could be tender and, beyond every other lesson he could teach us, that there was no shame in letting the tears run down our cheeks.

He had but to raise his voice to catch us with the percussively insistent beat of the male; but he could not have held us for so long too if we had not also heard in him a cry like a woman's. The force of the command was never so loud as to still the hurt of the plea; he could overbear and be overborne in the same phrase; the urgings of desire never traveled apart from the entreaty for love.

The old Cafe Society Downtown was the steadiest New York lodging of his first bloom, and I heard him there night after night without ever really managing to hear him at all. I hadn't the price for the tables and had to make do at the bar, which provided a splendid view of the back of his head and scarcely a sound from his throat. Somewhere on the road behind him, Joe Turner must have learned to focus his voice like a bullhorn with the loudest of messages for the faces in front and none for those behind.

My loss was small gain to my betters at the tables, where the whole of his range had narrowed. Most of their countenances were fixed in the opacity that reminds us how often in life those who might know cannot hear and those who can hear do not know. Cafe Society was a citadel of the Old Left and too many of its paying guests were too consciously aware of the miseries of African-American existence to reach out to a minstrel who sounded so little aware that he spoke as a man oppressed. And then the exuberance—indeed the sexual urgency—of his message had to put them off; they were not schooled enough in the complexities of Joe Turner's culture to catch the delicate notes beneath the coarse surface of its expression.

He did not fit their company but rather belonged to those places where the wantonly innocent come to play, in clubs populated by the young and the black, urban children now but still half-rural enough to hear the call of home when Joe Turner promised to hold them until the roosters crow for day. At Cafe Society he had only been passing through the first of his transient tenures in fashion; when it was over, he went unrepiningly back to those quarters where style endures, never lonely and never out of date.

M.K.

Joe Turner went to work for Atlantic Records in 1951 after a dreary Apollo Theater stint in Count Basie's service reminded him once again that the itinerant professional is never secure, even among those to whom he is most familiar. Ahmet Ertegun, lapsed graduate student, had come to him as an admirer with a business proposition that would provide Atlantic with its first creditable artistic asset. On his side, Turner had at hand no prospect more promising than self-indenture to this son of a Turkish diplomat; and he cast the same cheerful countenance upon the kindly stranger as he had once long before in Kansas City, when the just-as-unfamiliar John Hammond came so unexpectedly to fetch him back to New York, and to several sweet seasons in the Negro League of commercial recording.

Turner already knew Herb Abramson, the Erteguns' first Minister of Culture, who had recorded him in the mid-forties for National Records. Al Greene, National's proprietor, was a Detroit paint manufacturer who had begun making records so he could sell more varnish and was a pioneer among the culture gangsters who bought and sold black music in the immediate postwar era. Atlantic's founders were jazz collectors intruding notions of art into a business environment dominated by the mom and pop storekeepers, rack jobbers, and song pushers who had seized the means of record production as a sideline for their more permanent commercial interests, because they knew that black music was safe from the oligarchs of the commercial music establishment, whose contempt for the creators and the consumers of this stuff was as sovereign as their own. Most of them were selling a product they would never have brought into their own homes. They had thus no urge to improve it; and so they became an unconscious medium of a cultural exchange among aliens, undisturbers of a tradition they exploited but never cared to own.

But the original Atlantic group was comprised of enthusiasts who had in younger days forayed into neighborhoods where their parents suggested they didn't belong to buy records their parents thought beneath their attention, and who believed that, if this music had so compelled them, others of their kind could be persuaded to follow if only the music could be rendered more accessible. To sell the music was to take it to degrees that they had not until then imagined. But like all those who love too closely and too well, they could not venerate the object of their devotion quite long enough to suppress the itch for improving its character. Perhaps the integrity of a tradition is better preserved in the indifferently rough hands of savages who don't know its worth than in the tenderest care of curators who mistake their appreciation for proprietorship and, with all the assurance of wholesome intentions, cannot resist uprooting what they have found for the sake of making it better.

By 1953, two years after Joe Turner's enlistment, Herb Abramson had given the guidance of Atlantic's recording output over to Jerry Wexler, whose reputation as a sound and sensitive craftsman would later be brought close to a small legend's size by his association with Aretha Franklin. Wexler was a man of reliable instinct and considerable taste, prepared for the small sacrifices of both that the altars of commerce would demand if he was to bend the high priests of traditional blues who dominated Atlantic's earlier catalogs to the adjustments required to produce the hit records it had to have to survive.

By the time Wexler took charge, the basic elements of Joe Turner's style were as immutably a part of the nature of his environment as any rock or river formation could be of the ages that engraved it. His style had been shaped by female blues singers who had been coast-to-coast black entertainment stars in the twenties and thirties, mostly country-born and city-working with jazz pianists and six-piece bands. Aside from those white crooners whose influence on their African-American contemporaries cannot be discounted, the secular male voices most familiar to Turner would have belonged to those Southern primitives. But they could teach him far more of the lexicon of the standard blues idiom than about how to convey it in ways satisfactory to himself, because neither the abjection nor the ferocity that run as alternating currents through so much country blues was compatible with his nature.

It isn't surprising then that a man who in time to come would create one of the definitive masculine styles in black music took most of his schooling from women singers. He adored Ethel Waters, and the refinement that lives so singularly with the occasional coarseness of his language was achieved by protracted study of her diction. He learned much about phrasing from her, even while he was pushing past such formal conventions as her practice of putting the words right on the beat. In his earlier records he indulged few of these liberties; his cadences sound more carefully measured, his delivery so much more mannered as almost to mince in comparison to the mature style he arrived at in the early forties when he became Big Joe Turner for real.

The voice seems lighter too on those first records, although its extraordinary resonance clamored in the memory of everyone who had been witness to his beginnings as a singing bartender in Kansas City. Part of Turner's job then was to stand on the Reno Club's sidewalk and draw a crowd, and it is said his unamplified voice could carry for five blocks. He would be classified ever after as a blues shouter, a characterization altogether inappropriate for the subtleties of his attack. We do not speak of opera singers as shouters because they sing loud—and Jerry Wexler always said Joe Turner could have sung opera.

By the time Turner came to Wexler's hands his voice had rung its changes through material of merits so uneven that it had become almost a force of nature, able to blow away any clutter that sloppy or bad judgment might put in its path. Two of the latest among these challenges had been constructed by Ahmet

Count Basie and his orchestra swung the blues like no one.

Ertegun himself: one a lugubrious ballad called "Chains of Love," whose country-and-western inflections prefigured the calculated leap and well-cushioned fall into banality that Ray Charles would undertake a decade or so later, and the other, "Sweet Sixteen," an earnest but derivative blues that made a lot of money for Atlantic in 1952 and much more for B. B. King when he appropriated it as his own in 1960.

"Chains of Love" and "Sweet Sixteen" had brought Turner a grander commercial success than his recordings ever had before. Still, they could scarcely serve as prototypes for the modernized package that Atlantic wanted for him. Wexler and the Erteguns were already charting the passage between them and a crossover into the white market.

The wartime swelling of upsouth migrations had pushed millions of African-Americans into Northern cities and shifted the balance of the black population from country to town; and, when the fifties opened, town seemed suddenly crowded with people who hadn't been there long enough to cast off the outlook and tastes that country life had bred in them. By then these new arrivals had grown to a critical mass in an expanding black marketplace, and independent record companies proliferated in urban centers from New York to Chicago and Memphis, catering to the appetites of these migrants for music made by people like them and meant for people like them.

Joe Turner was born to the city and, as a representative of its established culture and settled tastes, he found himself rather a stranger in the floodtide of the freshly-come. He had label-hopped through the late forties while the merchants of schlock and shellac who held control of his exiguous recording career struggled to adjust themselves to customers whom the profit motive obliged them to take seriously but whose desires they were unable to distinguish from those they had previously served and could not recognize as irrelevant to the commanding impulses of an altered marketplace. Ready as Joe Turner may have been to break the new furrows, the hands that owned the ploughs were as cold as a corpse's even while the clouds around them grew heavy.

The first five postwar years were a time of feverish change in the popular music of African-Americans, but Joe Turner's workplace was still Lucky Millinder's and Wynonie Harris's and especially Louis Jordan's world; he just floated there while new currents divided the mainstream into several tributaries of which his was the smallest and the slowest-moving. He had, after all, never really been a recording star, even though his 1939 "Cherry Red" had stimulated the music

Jimmy Rushing, the

great blues shouter of

the Kansas City

tradition who came to

fame with the

Count Basie Band.

business's grander enterprisers to take a more emphatic account of the profits hidden in what they called the "race" market than they had since Mamie Smith's "Crazy Blues" had first brought it to their attention eighteen years before.

The middle-aged Joe Turner's summertime began in 1953 when the principals of Atlantic decided to record him on the road, where he was grinding away in the entourage of Paul Williams the Hucklebuck King. The choice of venue was dictated partly by the stubbornness of the artist and almost as much by the shrewdness of his new patron. Turner had a commitment to steady work anywhere Joe Glaser's Associated Booking could find to send him; he'd be reluctant to interrupt the rhythms of a regular paycheck by traveling to New York on an invitation full of promise and apparently empty of guarantees.

But then Ahmet Ertegun had already observed to Art Rupe, proprietor of Specialty Records's Los Angeles base and its flourishing New Orleans outpost, that Rupe was lucky he could record in cities where the things he wanted came naturally to musicians, while Atlantic had to use New York jazzmen and make them copy styles indigenous elsewhere. Rupe had only to trust in found objects to unfold the authentic style for him; Ertegun had first to locate the elements of authenticity he needed for commercial purposes and then re-create them by consciously subverting the sophistication native to his own environment.

In 1953, Ertegun recorded Turner in New Orleans with a local band. What he got was a Turner dressed up in the exuberance of New Orleans, a raucous cartoon of masculine aggression that appealed to the adolescent posturings of men of all ages. "Honey Hush" came very near to being the biggest record in black America that year, anticipating "Shake Rattle and Roll," just around the corner.

A few months later Jerry Wexler recorded Turner in Chicago; as Turner recalled ten years afterwards, "They wanted a real funky guitar so they come up with Elmore James." James would later became the hero of a posthumous minor cult whose devotees, addled by the romance of his obscure Mississippi origins, a vagrant life, and early death, worshiped him as the bearer of Robert Johnson's flame. But James was in truth only a one-lick guitarist of the upsouth Chicago school, with limited fluency in his idiom, a voice between a crack and a croak, and a single chord, insistent, bent and jangled, as specifically his as his thumbprint. And in further truth, Joe Turner made the best Elmore James and, in its way, perhaps the best blues record ever. "TV Mama" was born on October 7, 1953, harbinger of the style that would define the future of rock and roll.

Now and then an artist will stop in at the workshop of an artisan and make from the mere stuff at hand the distinguished thing that separates the extraordinary from the routine. "TV Mama" marked one of those times. There is indeed more of this record in white rock's final development than the supposedly more seminal "Shake Rattle and Roll"; those, particularly the British, who started the currents that would turn into the mainstream of the sixties borrowed less from Turner than from the Chicago blues tradition. We have only to hear Turner casually toss off "Oh … she's mighty fine … lovely picture" as punctuation to Elmore James's "TV Mama" solo to discern the threads of attitude that Mick Jagger would pick up and embroider into the persona that would be an essence of the contemporary popular culture.

"Shake Rattle and Roll" has been assigned a probably undeserved importance as an aboriginal rock and roll number, mostly because a Delaware hillbilly band's speckled dog of a cover version captured white children everywhere and made Bill Haley a star. The Turner original's real distinction may instead abide in its introduction of the rock and roll hook, a punchline phrase that ingrains itself and closes the sale. This innovation can be credited to Jesse Stone, a pianist who, like Turner, had flowered in Kansas City a quarter century before and had since been transplanted to New York, to be cultivated by Ahmet Ertegun as the house arranger who would make his dreams of the crossover come true.

In February of 1954 Joe Turner and Jessie Stone, who must have known each other of old, joined in making "Shake Rattle and Roll." Stone wrote it in the tradition of Turner's own casually crafted, open-ended, recurrent variations of the same old song, and then loaded it up with a phrase of special purpose, a punchline that stood out against the internal logic of the song's text like neon on a dark night, words whose resonance is so powerfully amplified as to become what is first and best remembered. The hook, a device adapted from the advertising copywriter's toolbox, gave "Shake Rattle and Roll" its pop identity, a singsong suitable for singalong. Once converted to the uses of Bill Haley and his Comets, it became rock and roll. And Turner rode that song the way he had ridden all the others on all the bad tracks in all the bad years and good ones and those in between, and like a jockey, he just sat in the middle and rocked it from side to side, rode it so hard that he got anointed by *Cashbox Magazine* as "the most popular rhythm and blues artist of 1954." At forty-three, Joe Turner was suddenly reborn into the business of selling to the young. In the still rigidly segregated music industry of the early fifties, Big Joe Turner was briefly a big black star.

But by the reckoning of his overseers, Turner's rich and experienced intuition had become an impediment to fulfilling his potential in the world of wider commercial possibilities that had opened before them. He had followed blind street singers around Kansas City as a child, he had hungrily studied in the neighborhood record shops that were the libraries of his youth, he had been throwing down in adult venues when he was thirteen years old, and singing had been his only job in life. He had made himself so entire a dictionary of the language of thirty years of African-American popular song that one night in Los Angeles, he was said to have sung the same song for forty-five minutes and never repeated a verse.

But for Jerry Wexler and Ertegun, the trick was to get Joe to sing some new lyrics, something other than "eyeslikediamondsteethshinelike Klondikegold"; and so, especially after "Shake Rattle and Roll," they gave him other people's songs to sing. Since Turner couldn't read much, Atlantic tried teaching him with demonstration records. Whatever the company made for him Turner did his best to deconstruct, converting the process of learning a song somebody else had written into the more familiar process of creating one of his own. When they gave him "Boogie Woogie Country Girl," for example, he later said, "I walked down the street and sang it to myself, I'd take it home to the hotel, lay down and listen to it, put the TV on awhile, go in a bar and drink a little wine, come back, go down the street again, look around, go downtown to a picture show, bump around all over New York, all the time singing the song, I call Atlantic and tell 'em I'll be ready in a coupla days."

Atlantic, then, made out of Turner an approximate self, better suited to the market than the real one. Thus a line like Turner's "You so evil you'd throw a rock at a hearse" would be gentled by Stone into "I believe in my soul you're the devil in nylon hose," suggesting a calculated solicitude for transforming every genuine complaint into the playful pretense of exasperation. "Flip Flop and Fly" came next as the follow-up that signified Turner's official lodgment in the pop music chain. When he sang it he sounded as if he were focusing on something in the middle distance—suddenly aware of people paying attention whom he'd never noticed before, and who would expect him to compose himself. As soon as he recognized that he had to put some distance between the self and the material, he caught his stride as a pop singer and was given new material from which he was even more easily distanced, since it had been crafted by the Liebers, the Stollers, the Doc Pomuses, and other adherers to Ahmet Ertegun's now established precept that "watered down blues was all the white kids could swallow."

"Corrine, Corrina," Turner's last hit for Atlantic, so devoutly acknowledged pop's current conventions as to embrace one of their tawdriest, the MitchMillerized chorale that was then a prescribed dosage for flavoring ethnic music to white folks' taste. After that, Atlantic ran out of ideas for keeping Turner in the mainstream, shifted its concentration to new discoveries, and effectively retired him as a pop singer.

Jerry Wexler, who was a truly hope-to-die acolyte, knew how much he had had to debase Turner's style to widen its market, and had excused himself with the promise that some day he would make the record he really wanted to make. The Joe Turner record Wexler really wanted to make was "Boss of the Blues." He called Pete Johnson in, backed them both with a distinguished cadre of Basie and Ellington veterans, and directed their attention to the staples of Turner's Kansas City songbook. The quality of what they all produced was so surpassing that if "Boss of the Blues" were all we were ever to have of Joe Turner it would have been all we'd ever need. The money in the till and little prospect of more, the producer's statement finally made, and the singer's opportunity for the true expression of his art and his craft finally secured, Joe Turner passed quickly and quietly into the Atlantic Records Hall of Fame. His voice lived on in its splendor for another twenty-eight years, while he fought back the ailments that stole progressively more of his physical health and at last took his life in 1985.

A.K.

"The Boss of the Blues" broke into my consciousness when Joe Turner had all but left it; now that he had brought back the epitome of what I had loved and forgotten, I took to tendering it for weddings and birthdays and other occasions that demanded modest tokens of hope and affection. It was indeed the all-we-could-ever-need-to-know, but there was a smell of the embalmer in my paradings of this saint's head in its reliquary. He had stopped being a live presence for me except at junctures when I would now and then struggle to check some wild lurch of my own language into the thickets of mannerism and grasp for that voice of his that strikes every syllable like a hammer. I would fix on, say, "She's yours she's mine, she's somebody else's too" and, often as of old, it would work me back to the beat.

But then, late in the seventies, Barney Josephson brought Joe Turner back to the Village and his image rose again in my mind—not dead and, praise God, not even martyred—and I went looking for him before it would be too late for either or both of us. By then he had swelled twice over with poundage that must have been mostly water and he could not stand for longer than a minute or so, and he walked as elephants are said to on the way to their graveyard. Nothing remained of his used-to-be except its instrument and that was as full, fresh, and resonant as when he first set to calling the children home forty-five years before.

The widenings and elevations of the soul were his to dispense as prodigiously as ever, but you could not give way to them undistracted by the puzzle of why he went on enduring the pains of the flesh they so plainly cost him. He had always been a steady and sober workman; even if he hadn't been, his royalties from ASCAP and the dozen of his yet-extant albums ensured that he need flog himself no further.

I did not begin to understand this endurance of ordeals sure to kill him before California's quietude could until my last pilgrimage to Tramps, a Manhattan East Side bar of the unbuttoned and unassuming ambience now slipping into the mists of time. The house band had been meeting its responsibilities in a fashion suggestive of strangers too world-weary to improve an unwelcome acquaintance. And then Joe Turner was fairly carried to the stand, stretched legs feeble as a baby's, snapped his fingers once or twice, and launched into "Roll 'Em Pete"; and suddenly the band reared up and rolled straight ahead in the surprise of being together and driving and driven by this great voice.

These sidemen had been sitting behind that back of his which had walled me away from the sound of him at Cafe Society long ago and which must be presumed to be working its same bafflements upon them now. And yet they had roused and cut loose at a summons perhaps inaudible to those of us who had been beguiled by the beat when we were young, but loud and clear to those poor souls who had been so caught up, bound and trussed up by it as to condemn themselves to a life term and who had almost forgotten it in the protractions of their servitude but still had only to hear a whisper of the beat to be called back to what they had begun being and hoping to better be.

Two women in attendance that night said that Joe Turner looked as though he had never in his whole life been this bored. It is too true indeed that, even while the old urgings to "Blow the horn, boys, Blow the horn loud"

rang glad as always, fleshly misery had engraved his face with the stolidity that announces the Olmec god's awareness that death is beating at his door. But the look was not boredom but the concentrated ferocity of the knowledge that he hadn't many nights left for picking up and waving like a banner. His resources did not extend to entertainment; his audience was not Tramps's paying guests but these horns, this bass, this piano, and these drums; and all the reserves of his energy were being spent to compel them into a communion to which the rest of us were only spectators in a game that you had to play to be part of.

Big Joe Turner

(facing page)

He was at once together with his lessers still alive and alone with his ghosts. So what if Pete Johnson was dead? Joe Turner would create a Pete Johnson in a piano player who had long since ceased imagining he ever could be.

Perhaps I was wrong to read so much into this scene; to infer that Joe Turner endured his joy-embued torments to proclaim that the whole great point of life is to stay what you were and in the company of all the departed who were with you when you were young. But right or wrong, I shall always believe that Joe Turner was truly at home not, as Norman Granz so devoutly misapprehended, with Basie or Gillespie or Eldridge, but with rags, tags, and bobtails like the ones Tramps had served him for lifting beyond themselves. He belonged with the Fender basses and the electric guitars; like muddlers of the stream he had only to shout to clear and wake the young who did not know to rock as they never had before, and would not in his absence soon rock again. That supreme gift to the young was, I suppose, Joe Turner's reason to suffer and stay alive. And the memory of the night I watched him still doing it so near the end remains with all the memories of other men and women I have seen at moments when they held steadfast to the command to glory and instructed and consoled a heart wearied with the long waiting to see their like again.

M.K.

MUDDY WATERS

GONE TO MAIN STREET

by Pete Welding

When I sing the blues, when I'm singing the real blues, I'm singing what I feel. Some people maybe want to laugh; maybe I don't talk so good and they don't understand, you know? But when we sing the blues—when I sing the blues, it come from the heart. From right here in your soul, an' if you' singing what you really feel it comes out all over. It ain't just what you saying—it pours out of you. Sweat runnin' down your face.

—MUDDY WATERS, AS TOLD TO PAUL OLIVER

Anyone who's followed the course of modern popular music is aware of the vast influence exerted on its development by the large numbers of blues artists who collectively shaped and defined the approach to amplified music in the late forties and early fifties. While it's true that the postwar electric blues came to flower in a score of cities simultaneously, Chicago easily takes pride of place for both the great quantity and high quality of the records its resident bluesmen produced in those exciting times. From the very beginning they were the tastemakers of the new music: their records literally set the pace for the modern blues styles, and it's no accident their hometown lent its name to the new blues. In the Chicago blues records of the period were laid out the basic ensemble practices and textures, as well as the individual instrumental approaches that quickly crystallized as the idiom's conventions. Truly Chicago was the pivotal point for the development and dissemination of the modern blues; virtually everything else has flowed, in one way or another, from this rich source.

The revolution began inauspiciously enough in 1948 with the release of a 78-rpm single by a singer-guitarist called Muddy Waters. Coupled on Aristocrat 1305 were a pair of traditional Mississippi Delta–styled pieces, "I Can't Be Satisfied" and "I Feel Like Going Home," and on them Waters's dark, majestic singing was supported—perfectly—by his equally brilliant electrified slide guitar and the percussive bass of Ernest "Big" Crawford. The record was a hit, selling rapidly to black audiences in the urban North and in the South who shared Waters's southern rural upbringing. This audience responded immediately to his music: it had the affirming familiarity that is one of the great strengths of all traditional utterance, yet at the same time it was thrillingly different. Waters's use of amplification gave his guitar playing a new, powerful, striking edge and sonority that introduced to traditional music a sound its listeners found very exciting, comfortably familiar yet strangely compelling and, above all, immensely powerful, urgent. Over the next several years he and hundreds of other country-cum-city bluesmen all over the nation were to extend and redefine traditional Southern blues into the postwar urban ensemble blues styles.

Nowhere was the activity more pronounced or the results more successful than in Chicago. The city early had been established as the most important Northern focus of Southern migration, and from the turn of the century vast numbers of Southern blacks had made their way there in the hopes of improving their lot. As a result a large and busy professional and semiprofessional music scene had grown to serve the needs of this segment of the city's populace, with large numbers of clubs, taverns, speakeasies and dance spots scattered through the

Muddy Waters

(facing page)

South and West Side black ghettos. The city's preeminence in black popular music was further consolidated when the large record firms of the twenties and thirties established the bulk of their activities in so-called race recording there, which made Chicago even more of a mecca for the Southern blues musician.

As a result of the major record firms' concentration of recording activities in one city, coupled with the rise of what might be considered a bloc of reliable, versatile studio musicians who in varying combinations performed on by far the major portion of the blues records made there, the Chicago blues recordings of the period 1935–45 tended toward a type of polished regularity that was suave and supple at best, bland and predictable at worst. Closed as this self-perpetuating studio blues scene was to new ideas, stagnation inevitably set in and the way was paved for the new synthesis of country and city that Waters and his followers set in motion right after the war. To serve the needs of the community in which it is rooted, a traditional music such as blues must look to the present, not to the past, and much of the music produced by the Chicago blues performers of the prewar and war years had become irrelevant to black audiences of the time. This was even more true of postwar black audiences, swelled as they were by Southern blacks who had come North to staff the industries of the booming wartime economy. Muddy Waters and his strong, yeasty music touched their hearts and minds, tapped into memories, much more deeply and immediately. Like them he had only lately arrived in the city from the rural South. His values, attitudes, experiences, and responses, as voiced in his music, were their own and they made him, and others like him, their spokesmen.

From the start it was he who dominated the music, who led the way—in style, sound, repertoire, instrumentation, in every way—first as a greatly popular club performer from the mid-forties on and, a few years later, as the most influential recording artist in the new amplified blues idiom. In the years 1948–55 he put forth for definition the fundamental approaches and usages of modern blues in a remarkable series of ground-breaking and, as time has shown, classic records. In the years since, the style Waters delineated has been extended, fragmented, elaborated, and otherwise commercialized, but the fundamental earthy, vital, powerful sound of the postwar blues as defined by Muddy and his bandsmen has yet to be excelled—or even equaled, come to that. It's no accident that the Rolling Stones chose their name from one of Waters's finest early recordings: the choice was merely prophetic, for Muddy and his magnificent bedrock music continue to resonate as thrillingly and powerfully through the music of today as they did back in the late forties and early fifties when we first heard them.

He was born McKinley Morganfield—Muddy Waters is a nickname given him in childhood—in the tiny hamlet of Rolling Fork, Mississippi, on April 4, 1915, but from the age of three, when his mother died, was raised by his maternal grandmother in Clarksdale, a small town one hundred miles to the north. "I went to school," he told Paul Oliver, "but they didn't give you too much schoolin' because just as soon as you was big enough you get to workin' in the fields. I guess I was a big boy for my age, but I was just a boy and they put me to workin' right along side the men. I handled the plough, chopped cotton, did all of them things."

Music served to lighten the workload, he observed. "Every man would be hollerin' but you didn't pay that no mind. Yeah, course I'd holler too. You might call them blues but they was just made-up things. Like a feller be workin' or most likely some gal be workin' near and you want to say somethin' to 'em. So you holler it. Sing it. Or maybe to your mule or something, or it's gettin' late and you wanna go home. I can't remember much of what I was singin' now 'ceptin' I do remember I was always singin' I cain't be satisfied, I be all troubled in mind. Seems to me like I was always singin' that, because I was always singin' jest the way I felt, and maybe I didn't exactly *know* it, but I jest didn't like the way things were down there—in Mississippi."

Certainly there was little to like in the way of life the cotton-producing Mississippi Delta offered the black farm laborer. Grinding poverty, perpetual hunger, poor health and disease, rudimentary educational opportunities, systematically administered brutality, more than occasionally murder—all have been the concomitants of the life of victimization, intimidation, and morally and physically debilitating servitude with which the System has held the Delta black in thrall since Emancipation. It was so when Waters was growing up in Mississippi in the twenties and thirties, and persisted well beyond this time. As recently as the sixties, for example, more than 80 percent of Mississippi black families were subsisting on less than $3,000 *family* income annually. Since 1946 the infant mortality rate among Mississippi blacks—then the nation's highest—has gone up almost steadily. And with increased technology—which in past years had made little inroads on the Delta cotton farms but which in recent years has been accelerated in face of competition from elsewhere in the U.S. and abroad—more than half the area's force of black farm laborers has been idled.

It is scarcely surprising then that the Delta region has nurtured a tradition of blues singing and playing that reflects the harsh, brutal life there, a music shot through with all the agonized tension, bitterness, stark power,

and raw passion of life lived at or near the brink of despair. Poised between life and death, the Delta bluesman gave vent to his terror, frustration, rage, and passionate humanity in a music taut with dark, brooding force and spellbinding intensity— jagged, harsh, raw as an open wound, and profoundly, inexorably, moving. The great Delta blues musicians—Charley Patton, Son House, Tommy Johnson, Garfield Akers and, especially in Waters's case, the brilliant, tortured Robert Johnson—sang with a naked force, majesty, and total conviction that make their music timeless and universal in its power to touch and move us deeply. That same power is present, in greater or lesser degree, in the work of all musicians who have come from the region. Such is the strength of the region's musical traditions that any singer who has been reared in the Delta carries its impress forever in the lineaments of his music.

Growing to manhood there, in the very heart of the region that had spawned this magnificent music, Waters was drawn early to its stark, telling, expressive power. He had been working as a farm laborer for several years when at thirteen he took up the harmonica, the instrument on which many blues performers first master the music's rudiments. "I was messing around with the harmonica ever since I got large enough to say, 'Santy Claus, bring me a harp.' But I was thirteen before I got a real good note out of it, before I started getting into the way of playing blues on harp. I started blowing and I learned how to blow a few things on that, and I got to be pretty good with that. No one showed me nothing; I got it myself."

Four years later he made the switch to guitar. He was taught the basics of the instrument and the region's characteristic way of using it by a close friend, Scott Bohanna (or Bowhandle), who was a year or two older. Shortly thereafter, Waters recalled, "I got to be a better guitar player than he was. In a year's time I could beat him playing. Bottleneck style 'most all the time. You see, I was digging Son House and Robert Johnson." The two were the undisputed masters of the region's characteristic "bottleneck" style of guitar accompaniment. (The method is so termed because the neck of a glass bottle is slipped over a finger of the guitarist's left, or "fretting" hand and slid over the strings of the instrument, which when struck by the right hand produce a whining, keening sound much like a cry.) With this technique the Delta bluesman could utilize the guitar as a perfect extension of his voice, the sliding bottleneck matching the dips, slurs, sliding notes and all the tonal ambiguity of the voice as it is used in singing the blues.

Describing these early experiences, Waters told Oliver: "Seems like everybody could play some kind of instrument, and there were so many fellers playin' in the jukes around Clarksdale, I can't remember them all. But the best we had to my ideas was Sonny House. He came from a plantation east of Clarksdale, Marks or Lambert way I think. [House was born in Lyon, Mississippi.] He used to have a neck of a bottle over his finger, little finger, touch the strings with that and make them sing. That's where I got the idea from. You break it off, hold it in a flame until it melts and gets smooth. He made some good records, you know, Sonny, but to my ideas he never did sound so good on record as he did when you heard him."

Pepper's Lounge on

Chicago's South side.

(following overleaf)

Waters studied House's music closely, for as he explained to Don DeMichael, "One night we went to one of these Saturday night fish frys, and Son House was there playing. I was using the bottleneck because most of the Delta people used this bottleneck-style thing. When I heard Son House I should have broke my bottleneck because this other cat (Bohanna) hadn't learned me nothing! Son House played this place for about four weeks in a row, and I was there every night...you couldn't get me out of that corner, listening to him, what he's doing. Years later, down around 1937—I was very good then, but I hadn't been exposed to the public—I heard this Robert Johnson come out, and he got his teaching from Son House. He had a different thing. Where we'd play it slow, Robert Johnson had it up-tempo. The young idea of it, y'know what I mean? I didn't know Johnson much; I saw him one time in Friars Point, Mississippi. I knew Son House very, very good."

Waters characterized his own approach as a combination of these two influences, plus what he brought to the synthesis. "So if you say I try to play like Son House—sure, I'm glad of that 'cause Son was a great man. Robert Johnson was one of the greatest there's ever been. So that makes me feel proud, 'cause I got my pattern from them. I can't go around it too far because I got to come back around to something in that particular field. Between the three of us, I'm doing Muddy Waters, but because I use a slide, I can't get away from the sound of those two people 'cause they made it popular years and years ago."

Within a year, Waters recalled, he had mastered the bottleneck style and the jagged, pulsating rhythms of Delta guitar. He had learned to sing powerfully and expressively in the tightly constricted, pain-filled manner that characterized the best Delta singers. By the time a team of Library of Congress field collectors headed by Alan Lomax visited and recorded Waters for the library's folksong archives in 1941 (they were looking for Robert Johnson at the time, unaware of his death three years earlier), returning to record him further the following year, he had had several years' local performing experience behind him. "He played all around our little town," the singer recalled. "We played all the different things around—Saturday

night suppers and Sunday afternoon get-togethers, even played for white get-togethers, picnics and such. It was a cotton farming area and, working out on a farm, you don't have too many 'cabaret nights.' Saturday night is your big night. I worked on the farms, I worked in the city, and I worked all around."

Providing the musical impetus for dancers at rough-and-tumble back country dances, in juke joints, and at picnics, house parties, and other rural entertainments had sharpened the young bluesman's vocal and instrumental abilities to a keen edge. Fourteen recordings were made by the Library of Congress field team—four performances by the Son Sims Four, a country string band of which Waters was a regular member, and ten Waters solo performances, of which four have second guitar in accompaniment to his strong lead. These discs reveal a performer whose singing and playing, while obviously but not slavishly modeled on Robert Johnson, are strong, individualistic, marvelously detailed and mutually complementary. "I Be's Troubled," "You Got To Take Sick and Die Some of These Days," two versions of "Country Blues" (based on Johnson's "Walking Blues"), "Why Don't You Live So God Can Use You?," "I Be Bound To Write to You," and "You're Gonna Miss Me When I'm Dead and Gone," very clearly reveal the dominance of Johnson's music on Muddy's. Just as clearly, the recordings show the strikingly distinctive power of the young Waters, both as singer and master of Delta bottleneck guitar. But then, Waters was twenty-seven years of age and had been performing for more than half of them.

The following year Muddy put the Delta behind him forever. He moved to Chicago in 1943, and never looked back. "I wanted to get out of Mississippi in the worst way," he told writer Peter Guralnick. "Go back?! What I want to go back for? They had such as my mother and the older people brainwashed that people can't make it too good in the city. But I figured if anyone else was living in the city, I could make it there too." The idea of making it through his music was very much in his mind for, as he told me, "I always thought of myself as a musician. The jobs I had back in Clarksdale and so forth, they were just temporary things. If I wasn't a good musician then, I felt that sooner or later I would be a good musician. I felt it in me. A little later I moved to Chicago. I was thinking to myself that I could do better in a big city. With my singing and the type of guitar I was playing, in my mind I thought I could do better. I could make more money, and then I would have more opportunities to get into the big record field."

It was not as easy in the Windy City as the young bluesman had imagined. It was the middle of the war and, though times were flush and there was a great deal of money to be earned in the defense industries, the winds

of change were blowing uncertainly through the music world. The Petrillo ban on recording was resulting in a decline in influence of the big bands, a tendency that was to accelerate sharply as the decade advanced. The antics of the beboppers were beginning to command attention in the press; the emergence of that revolutionary and uncompromising music signaled the mood of restlessness and discontent that was in the air.

At another level, the blues were at a crossroads, though few knew it at the time. The vigorous, country-based blues that Chicago had refined, polished, and institutionalized since the twenties, when the city had been established as the most influential blues recording center, had been progressively emasculated. The guts were gone. The once forceful, vital, and meaningful blues, which had spoken to and for two or more generations of black listeners, had been diluted by the large record firms to glossy, mechanical self-parody and tasteless double-entendre. The blues that Waters found on his arrival was as well-turned and sophisticated as it often was empty of genuine emotion or true relevance.

Walter Horton

"The big men around town singing the blues," Muddy recalled, mentioning several of the more authentic practitioners of the hard-core blues to be heard in wartime Chicago, "were Tampa Red, Big Maceo, Memphis Slim, and Sonny Boy Williamson—not Rice Miller, I mean the one that got killed. The original Sonny Boy it was…I worked on the West Side in a few taverns, and I played house parties too. I worked for a while with pianist-singer Eddie Boyd. He was here when I came and we is off-cousins, Eddie and myself. But he couldn't stand my playing because he wanted me to play like Johnny Moore, which I wasn't able to play. He wanted it to be a kind of sweet blues."

During the war years a great wave of northward migration had brought thousands of blacks from the rural South to staff the war industries in the urban centers: the steel mills and foundries of Gary, the automotive plants of Detroit and Flint, and the hundreds of heavy and light industries in the Chicago area. So vast was this northward wave, in fact, that almost 50 percent of the total movement of Southern blacks to the North in the century's first half took place in the years 1940–47.

With few exceptions there was little with which they could identify in most of the blues releases the major record firms dispensed with such monotonous regularity through the mid-forties. Slowly the big companies lost ground. They had completely misjudged the new blues audience, if in fact they even

Little Walter

knew of its existence. They had failed to take into account its new mood of restlessness and aggressiveness. As the war ended and the country began to return to the business of peacetime, the large recording monopoly was effectively at an end, at least as far as the black record-buying public was concerned.

The postwar years saw the emergence of a new blues style that more accurately mirrored the quick, exciting tempo of life in the urban North, a music that was as harsh and pungent and ruthless as life in the teeming black ghettos of Chicago, Gary, Detroit, Flint, Indianapolis. Producing the new blues were a host of small, independent record firms that, if not black-owned, were at least black-oriented in terms of the artists and idioms they recorded: Aristocrat/Chess/Checker, Savoy, King, Aladdin, Modern/RPM, and many others.

Spearheading the new blues was Waters. He had persevered with his music. After several years of playing to slowly increasing audiences, first at house parties and later in small taverns dotted throughout Chicago's huge, sprawling South and West Side black-belt slums, he had begun to record. Ironically enough, it was for Columbia Records that he had made his first recordings as a

Chicago bluesman—three sides cut in 1947, with a five-piece band—in a style midway between the popular jump-blues of the wartime period and the true postwar idiom that he was to forge a scant year or so later. Unfortunately, the recordings were not issued, nor were those of Johnny Shines (recorded at the same time). Working as a truck driver, Waters had managed to persuade the operators of Aristocrat—later Chess—Records, a small, independent Chicago firm, to record him.

After several exploratory recordings made in the company of pianist Sunnyland Slim and bassist Ernest "Big" Crawford, which made absolutely no impression on the record-buying public, Waters suddenly scored with the single "I Can't Be Satisfied/I Feel Like Going Home." And it is with this record that the history of the modern Chicago blues properly begins. There were earlier records by amplified bluesmen, to be sure—Johnny Young, Little Walter, Othum Brown, and Johnny Williams—but the age of the postwar blues is properly ushered in with this 1948 Waters release, an overnight sensation and a huge hit. Based on the modest sales of Waters's several earlier releases, Aristocrat's Leonard and Phil Chess reportedly ordered a sensibly small initial pressing of the record, and were absolutely stunned when it sold out in less than twenty-four hours.

It was very important to Waters (no less than to the fledgling Aristocrat operation), for as he told Jim Rooney, "To get a name, you had to get a record. People lived right up under me, they didn't know who I was until I got a record out. Then they say, 'He live right there!'—got to get a record. I got a hit the first one I got. I calls it luck. It was a big blues seller amongst the black peoples." Trading on the success of the record, Waters over the next few years gathered around him a group of like-minded, country-reared musicians with whom he proceeded to make blues history.

The characteristic sound Waters and his bandsmen projected was loud, mean, and magnificent, with all the instruments save drums electrically amplified. The beat was slowed down and heavily emphasized, particularly at first, when Waters employed such relatively naive drummers as "Baby Face" Leroy Foster and Elgin Evans (or Edwards). The band's standard instrumentation was two guitars, acoustic bass, harmonica, and drums, with piano and electric bass added later.

Over the surging rhythmic momentum the group developed so effortlessly, Waters's dark-hued voice chanted the Mississippi blues of his boyhood. In his singing could be heard echoes of the great Delta singers he so admired. Robert Johnson's music, especially, is at the root of so many of Waters's early commercial recordings: "I Can't Be Satisfied," "I Feel Like Going Home," "Walkin' Blues," "Mean Red Spider," "Little Geneva," and "Kind Hearted Woman," among others. But even if the source of the music is not specifically Johnson, it is ultimately based in the traditional blues of his native Mississippi Delta, always the linchpin of Waters's approach to music, as attested by "Rolling Stone" and "Still a Fool" (both remarkable reworkings of the Delta standard "Catfish Blues"), "Standing Around Crying," "Rollin' And Tumblin'," "Honey Bee," "Baby Please Don't Go," "Smokestack Lightnin'," and

Sunnyland Slim helped

a young Muddy

Waters, just up from

the Delta, record

his first sides for the

Aristocrat label.

(facing page)

"My Home Is In The Delta"; "Bird Nest on the Ground," and "Country Boy," the latter two recordings from the late sixties; and from the early seventies, "Who's Gonna Be Your Sweet Man When I'm Gone," and "Can't Get No Grindin'," among many others.

"What it was that made our records different," Muddy said of these early efforts, "we would set down and we kept that Mississippi sound. We didn't do it exactly like the older fellows—just with no beat to it. We put the beat with it, put a little drive to it. It's like, I would say—when Blind Lemon Jefferson and them was making records, back then they changed [chords or phrases] whenever they get ready. We went to putting time with the stuff. I think Tampa Red, Maceo [Meriwether] and them, they were very 'timed-up' people too. We went to putting time to our lowdown Mississippi blues. We put a pretty good group together because we learned the beat, learned what the people's moving off of. Even if it's the blues, we still had to drive behind it."

Following his earliest recordings, made primarily of traditional Mississippi blues staples and his adaptations of them, often recorded at producer Leonard Chess's insistence solely with the accompaniment of bassist Crawford (the pairing that had proven so successful on "I Can't Be Satisfied"), Muddy slowly broadened the traditional base of his music to incorporate new instrumental sounds and textures. Memorable among these early efforts were the remarkable trio recordings with Little Walter on harmonica and Crawford on bass in support of his incisive amplified bottleneck guitar: "You're Gonna Need My Help," "Louisiana Blues," "Long Distance Call," "Howlin' Wolf" and "Too Young To Know," all dating from 1950 or early 1951 and all justly praised masterpieces of the postwar blues. Similar to these but substituting Elgin Evans's tough drumming for Crawford's slap-bass is the 1951 trio performance "She Moves Me." Also dating from 1951 are another set of trio performances, this time featuring either bass or drums and two guitars—"Honey Bee" and "Still A Fool"—with Little Walter as a marvelously responsive second guitarist. On all of these is to be heard Waters's gripping, magnificently expressive bottleneck guitar.

Waters's regular second guitarist during this period was the empathetic, almost telepathic Jimmy Rogers whose deft, rhythmically unerring playing was unparalleled in the modern blues. A member of Waters's working band from the late forties, he was not to make his appearance on a Waters record until the end of 1951, the same time pianist Otis Spann was added to the group's lineup for live performances (he didn't appear on its records until almost two years had elapsed, however). With him on board, the modern blues band format and sound was fully

Willie Dixon

settled, documented on such Waters band performances as "I Just Want To Make Love to You," "Hoochie Coochie Man" and "I Want You To Love Me" (1953), "I'm Ready" (1954), "Just To Be with You" (1956), and a host of others. In such fast-paced company, Elgin Edwards proved too inflexibly basic a drummer and from mid-1954 he was replaced first by the jazz-inflected Fred Below and from early the following year by the marvelous Francis Clay, the most accomplished and sympathetic of all the band's drummers.

With the ensemble finally settled, the final element was added in the form of veteran bassist Willie Dixon, whose abilities as a songwriter of proven talent, versatility, and audience-pleasing cleverness enabled Waters to achieve

Otis Spann, piano

and James Cotton,

harmonica.

even wider success through the many songs he wrote specifically for, and in some cases helped produce for, the singer-guitarist and his crack ensemble. A partial listing of these includes the aforementioned "Hoochie Coochie Man," "I Just Want To Make Love to You," and "I'm Ready" as well as "Don't Go No Farther," "I Love the Life I Live I Live the Life I Love," "Close to You," "You Shook Me," "You Need Love," "The Same Thing," and others. Dixon's clever, streetwise, often humorous lyrics helped Waters retain his older listeners and extend his audience to a younger generation of urban blacks to whom the country blues of the earlier stage of his career were of little real interest. Too, they pointed Waters in a different direction, and from the middle fifties his songwriting became almost wholly urban in character, many of his compositions taking their place alongside the best of Dixon's efforts in the genre, as for example "She's Nineteen Years Old," "Walkin' Thru the Park," "You Can't Lose What You Ain't Never Had," and the anthemic "Got My Mojo Working," among others.

The years after the war were uncertain and confused times at best, and Waters's recordings were among the few genuine touchstones of reality offered blacks by the record industry. With these songs, at least, they could identify; Waters was singing to and for them. Songs and performance style accurately reflected the harsh, fast-paced, often brutal life of the ghetto—a life where hunger, poverty, and death were never very far away and where pleasure was quickly and often perilously seized. With its strong, vibrant rhythm, heavily amplified instrumentation, and dark, declamatory vocal style, Waters's music was perfect for temporarily dancing away the stark realities of ghetto life.

All through the fifties Waters solidified and extended his initial success with a series of recordings, many of them absolutely brilliant and none less than satisfying, which firmly established his approach as the dominant postwar blues style. Countless groups emulated its brusque, rude force and thrilling sonorities though few were able to match the peerless ensemble integration it attained so consistently and effortlessly. Members of Waters's various bands—guitarists Jimmy Rogers, Luther Tucker, Sammy Lawhorn, Luther Johnson, and Luther Allison, harmonica players Little Walter Jacobs, Junior Wells, and James Cotton, pianists Otis Spann and Pinetop Perkins—left to strike out with bands of their own, spreading the Waters gospel further. Later generations of bluesmen took Waters's approach as their birthright: Buddy Guy, Magic Sam, Otis Rush, J.B. Hutto, Jimmy Dawkins, Earl Hooker, Hound Dog Taylor, Homesick James Williamson, and scores of others in Chicago; Eddie Kirkland, Baby Boy Warren, Washboard

Muddy Waters

(facing page)

Willie, and others in Detroit; Lightnin' Slim, Lonesome Sundown, Lazy Lester, Slim Harpo, and all the other Southern artists recording for Excello, and so on—all have been in Waters's debt.

Four decades and more later, the blues of postwar Chicago remain the standard-bearers, the yardstick by which all others have been and continue to be measured. Waters, his cohorts, and immediate followers had limned definitively the contours of the style, and it was they who extended and reworked the idiom, bringing it to its highest levels. The music's greatest achievements were shaped wholly in Chicago and the entire period—the late forties and early to middle fifties—was one of stylistic experimentation and consolidation, a time of great excitement and musical ferment. For that matter, all of Waters's great recordings had been made by 1958, and the revolution he had initiated ten years earlier had won all its aims. By the mid-fifties the style he had forged was virtually unchallenged in its domination of the black record market The new music had been the making of a number of record labels—Chess and Vee-Jay in Chicago, Excello in Nashville, Duke in Houston, and to a degree RPM/Modern in Los Angeles were among the most important, though there were others as well—and their emergence as important new outlets for the music of America's black subculture saw the pattern of record manufacture and distribution, formerly monopolized by a few major firms, enter a revolutionary new phase. The music was actively promoted over numbers of black radio stations that increasingly had served the needs of the subculture since the onset of World War II. And the stage was set for the music's next development, rock and roll and its offshoots and permutations.

And while it would be fatuous to suggest that this entire edifice stemmed from one man or one record, there can be little doubt that Waters and Aristocrat 1305 played their parts in the developments that followed. Muddy's emergence as a seminal contributor to the emerging postwar blues can be dated from the record's success, and this contributed not only to the furtherance of his own career and everything he accomplished in it, including all the musicians and songwriters whose careers he fostered over the years, but stimulated the further growth and prosperity of Chess Records.

As the fifties gave way to the sixties, blues of the direct, yeasty sort Waters and his bandsmen performed so tellingly became ever less relevant to black listeners who increasingly involved themselves with soul music and its offshoots, the more urbane blues styles of B. B. King and his disciples, and various forms of modern black dance music. In easing the transition from country to city

Muddy Waters

(facing page)

living, Waters's strong country-based music largely had served its purpose for blacks who shared with him a common background in the rural South but who, a decade or more later, had put these experiences behind them. Through the sixties sales of Waters's single releases had tapered off dramatically, and from the middle of the decade on most of his recordings took the form of albums.

By this time, however, Waters and other blues performers of his generation had been discovered and taken up by a new audience—young, white, and middle-class—born of the folk music revival of the late fifties and swelled even further a few years later by the British blues boom. The audience was large, enthusiastic, and affluent, and it took to Waters in a big way. The bars, taverns, and dance halls of the chitlin circuit in which he had performed for black dancers and listeners in the previous decade soon had given way to college auditoriums, folksong, blues, and jazz clubs, and festival stages, both here and abroad, increasing international touring, television appearances, and wide acceptance by the rock community, which accorded him the respectful adulation given a founding figure. And while he was confused and hurt by the defection of black listeners, and couldn't understand their turning away from the blues, Waters was nothing if not pragmatic. If he couldn't play for blacks any longer, why then he'd play for whites, for anyone who'd listen. He simply took things as they came, continued to be and play himself in his music. In Peter Guralnick's apt characterization, he was "a man who, like many another great artist seeking recognition as well as reward," was "forced to go outside of his own community to get it." In doing so, he simply enlarged his community, earning greater recognition and reward as a result. Far from losing anything, Waters gained through the transaction. And his young white listeners gained even more—the beauty and majesty of his music.

Through all this his mentors at Chess Records sought to keep pace with the changing tides in popular music, in response to which they placed Waters in a number of recording contexts they felt would broaden his acceptance even further. He was recorded with big-band accompaniment, in the company of a number of young British blues-based rockers, "live" at the chic Chicago supper club Mr. Kelly's, even in a "psychedelic" setting, and so on. The most sensitive and, happily, one of the best received of these productions was the two-LP set *Fathers And Sons*, which paid homage to Waters and his achievements through the sponsorship and participation of several young musicians who had learned directly from him, repaying the favor by using their celebrity to focus attention on him—the brilliant young harmonica player Paul Butterfield and guitarist Michael Bloomfield.

In 1977, his long association with Chess at an end, he signed with Blue Sky Records, a label operated by another of his young protégés, the guitarist and singer Johnny Winter, and over the next several years produced under Winter's sympathetic guidance four albums, of which the first, *Hard Again*, enjoyed a deserved success for its spirited return to basics, an approach followed in the others as well. During this period, he frequently toured with Winters.

Except for a period in the early seventies, when a long convalescence from a road accident curtailed his activities, Waters performed almost uninterruptedly, invariably giving of his best and often, when circumstances conspired to allow it, setting the night on fire with the strength, passion, and conviction that only he could muster. The quality of the bands he led in these years varied, and this had an effect on the music, but he himself remained unswervingly committed to, and approached with great seriousness, the music he had first been drawn to as a young fieldhand in Mississippi and which more than anything else he sought to master. He not only did this, but carried its message to countless listeners, first in Chicago, then all the rest of the U.S., and finally, the world. When he died quietly in his sleep on April 30, 1983, in his home in suburban Westmont, Illinois, America lost one of the greatest, most influential and enduringly important musicians of the century, one who had reshaped the course of the blues, set it on a new path, and, through the influence he exerted on so many others who followed in his trailblazing wake, completely altered the sound, substance, and very character of all modern popular music.

PROFESSOR LONGHAIR

DEEP SOUTH PIANO
AND THE BARRELHOUSE BLUES

by Robert Palmer

During the early seventies, when I was spending a lot of time in New Orleans, I found myself rooming down the hall from Professor Longhair. Fess was a legend, still more heard of than heard, and had just started performing again after a layoff of fifteen-odd years. He'd been supporting himself, after a fashion, as a card sharp, living hard, and it showed in his lined, weathered face. His "Go to the Mardi Gras" was a local jukebox favorite every year around carnival time, but apparently he'd never received any royalties.

Aside from that single the only available recording of his music was the Atlantic album, "New Orleans Piano," collecting his singles from the late forties and early fifties, and even that was hard to find.

Fess had recently returned to performing with a triumphant appearance at the New Orleans Jazz and Heritage Festival, but that was still a small, primarily local event, and other gigs were scarce. After the loss of his

house and everything in it, he was penniless. But I never heard a despairing word cross his lips, or detected a trace of bitterness. At our mutual friend's spacious old house near the French Quarter, he received a stream of visitors, all of them musicians, but musicians of many generations and persuasions. Drummer Zig Modeliste, then riding high with the Meters, visited frequently, and told me at one point, "Fess is the foundation of all New Orleans music since World War II. Every drummer who's made records or regular club gigs in this town has studied him."

One night Willie Tee (Turbinton), one of New Orleans' finest soul singers ("Teasin' You") and an all-around keyboard master equally at home with blues, classical music, and jazz, settled in for a powwow. He seemed genuinely thrilled when Fess suggested they play some four-handed piano on the battered old upright in our host's funky but comfortable basement rec room, and they jammed for hours. Not once did they clutter the music or get in each other's way. Fess chose the keyboard's bass end and provided tricky but clearly executed and rock-solid rhythm patterns—Afro-Cuban, walking basses, driving boogie-woogie. Tee embroidered modernist chord extensions, delicate filigree, and incisive push-pull counterrhythms, weaving them into the very fabric of Fess's fundamentals. The feeling in the little room was one of mutual respect and love, fierce concentration, and more than a little magic. When they'd finished, Fess asked Willie to play "Stormy Weather" for him, solo, and the rendition that emerged rang in the air; a phantasm of latticework harmonics emerged long after Tee removed his hands from the keyboard.

Late that night, the tinkling, insubstantial ghost of a sound woke me from a deep sleep, though the sound was too faint to hear clearly. I opened my door and tiptoed to the head of the stairs. It was Fess, two flights down, alone at the upright in the basement. He was playing some of the strangest music I had ever heard. The right-hand melodies and their bass-register underpinning strained to embrace each other, almost palpably yearning for union, yet the music's tenderness was more than matched by a fitful, bracing discord and unpredictably timed bursts of violent, jabbing frustration. After I'd taken a seat at the top of the stairs and spent some time with this perplexing, otherworldly night music, it finally sorted itself out in my mind and I "got" it. Fess was trying to play "Stormy Weather," but because he was so purely a bluesman, he was trying to fit the tune's harmonic modulations and serpentine melody into some sequence or combination of the tonic, subdominant, and dominant, the three chords that define the harmonic parameters of the blues. Of course it wasn't working, not in any conventional sense. Yet the effort was so noble, and the soundscape of grinding tonal collisions so expressive and fresh, it was much more than any perfectly articulated showpiece casually tossed off by a virtuoso. I must have listened for hours before I noticed my eyelids drooping and returned to bed, leaving the door open so that the music could insinuate itself into my dreams.

Before he became a New Orleans icon of near-mythic dimension Fess was simply Henry Roeland Byrd, born in Bogalusa, Louisiana, on December 19, 1918, and raised by his mother in New Orleans. His family was musical, and although his father left when he was young, his mother would organize family musicales with Henry and the other children, who played homemade instruments like comb-and-tissue-paper kazoos, washtub bass, and dime-store horns while mom, apparently a player of some accomplishment, picked guitar. By the time he was in his early teens, Henry was playing blues guitar himself, but the family was scuffling, and Henry did his part by dancing on street corners, often as part of children's groups that sang ragged harmony and played "spasm-band" music on toy instruments. In addition to dancing, Byrd played "percussion" using forks and spoons and occasionally played "drums" on orange crates and garbage cans, using brooms for brushes. When a parade or marching band came within earshot, Henry would take whatever he had to beat out a rhythm on and join the informal second line that followed the bands, contributing polyrhythms against the march cadences along with a considerable amount of sheer metallic noise.

New Orleans street rhythms, and especially the second line, worked their way out through Byrd's dancing and, later, his distinctive piano rhythms. "Second line music is strictly soul," he used to say. "If you've got a bucket, a bottle, or a pan, you're welcome to join in, if you can include the sound. Just don't mess up, 'cause those people can easily tell with their ears and point a cat out as making a bad note." Note? Throughout his life, Fess used the words note and beat interchangeably, suggesting a fundamental rule in the musical cosmos called the blues: if it sounds right and is sounded in the right place rhythmically, it isn't a wrong note, regardless of pitch.

It's common now to think of this as "oral tradition," but we're talking musical systems analysis here, and a strict education in the conservatory of the streets. Fall in with a bunch of apparently drunk and disorderly revelers, pick up a bottle and a stick, and join in. But put the wrong note in the wrong place and you're OUT. "In those days, the second line was a second *band*, in back of the first band," Longhair recalled fondly. "And," he insisted, "they'd actually be gettin' a better sound with their bottles and sticks and pieces of iron than the band got, 'cause most of the brass bands could only play two or three different numbers, over and over, and meanwhile them cats behind would be really ballin' with all that junk."

Fess was exposed to everything from ragtime to Dixieland to opera in addition to the rhythms of the streets, but the blues he encountered, and played on the guitar, seems to have been loosely-structured and improvisational, country-style. "There wasn't no certain time or air," he recalled. "It was different structures; you just produced a sound to fit the verses. But I didn't care for that feel. I'm ready for action; I like to be movin' all the time. Just let me around some way out beats, some *movements*."

When he was in his mid-teens, Byrd found a junked piano that had been abandoned in an alley near his home: "It was broken, but I bought some strings and hammers and just kept fumblin' and foolin' with it. I finally patched it up 'til one or the other key would play, even if four or five wouldn't. It didn't matter to me. I wanted to play so bad I'd just match 'em up and sound 'em off. That's when I started cross-chording the piano—putting alias keys in there to give it a better blend. Where you would use three keys, I might use the whole five. There's no tellin' how many times I'll hit one key doin' this; I couldn't count it but I can feel it. You've got so much space when you're playin' music. You can play in so much of that space, or you can roll over, as long as you can stay within that space and stay on that pitch"—here he illustrated "pitch" by snapping his fingers rhythmically. "See, I might do a thing and then do it *again*, to express my feelings and to let people know I'm not just simply luckin' up on this, I'm *executin'* it."

Up to this point, Byrd sounds like an utter maverick, drawing on the wealth of his musical influences around him but belonging to no known school or idiom. But he was growing, evolving, the tyro bluesman who hears and imitates field hollers; sings harder and with more melodic embroidery, hones his rhythmic sense in a country church; builds and masters a one-stringed diddley bow, tries his hand at harmonica or drums, and finally decides to get serious and learn guitar. Byrd gradually shed the skin of a talented young amateur and committed himself to "real" music. And like a country-bred bluesman, he understood that a serious musician needed a teacher, a guru. Fess found his teachers in back-of-town gin mills and bargain-basement whorehouses. They were not settled, urbane musicians; they were rambling bluesmen through and through.

The early blues pianists may not have been able to carry their instruments on their backs like guitars, but they traveled as widely and as frequently as their guitarist counterparts. Rocking, hard-driving rhythm patterns like boogie-woogie are associated with these pianists and assumed to have originated with them, but we really don't know for sure. Texas pianist Clay Custer's 1922 recording of "The Rocks" (pianists' slang for those driving bass patterns) is the first boogie-based blues on record. "Pinetop's Boogie-Woogie," recorded by Pinetop Smith in 1928, was the first boogie hit. But veteran Texas boogie-blues pianist Sammy Price remembers Blind Lemon Jefferson playing boogie bass on guitar, and singing about a jumping house party or "booger rooger," as early as 1911, some years before Price heard any pianist use the style. Since we'll never know who came first, we are left to sift through the little we do know about the origins of piano blues.

The guitarist's advantage was mobility; the pianist's advantage, in the years before amplification, was volume. Piano bluesmen couldn't and didn't wander indiscriminately; they traveled a well-worn circuit from lumber camps to turpentine camps to piano-equipped honky-tonks in cities and towns like New Orleans, Houston, Memphis, and Helena, Arkansas. Some wandered considerably farther, but the most important stimulus to the development of their art seems to have been the piney woods lumber and turpentine camps in Louisiana, Mississippi, and East Texas and the flimsy, impermanent oil-drilling boomtowns along the gulf coast. In many of these situations, the pianists literally played to a captive audience. Hired black laborers cleared the forests, chopped the lumber, tapped the remaining trees for turpentine, and finally burned off and cut back the stumps and remaining vegetation to make way for immense cotton plantations like those to the north and east. These laborers were nominally free agents, but they were working and living in hastily erected camps, often miles from any town or city, and subject to the disciplinary whims of their bosses and overseers. When payday came on Friday, the pay often came not in U.S. currency but in company scrip, which was legal tender only at company-owned establishments such as the rough gin mills that were the social center of every work camp. These joints were soon known as "barrelhouses," and they were usually large places, and loud places. One or even several guitarists would've been virtually inaudible. But a pianist with a strong left hand, a man who could pound out the "rocks" and keep 'em dancing, was welcome in any barrelhouse, and often finished a weekend with money in his pocket, if he finished it with life and limb intact.

Jelly Roll Morton enjoyed giving the impression that he was an uptown slickster, organizing jazz bands or composing when he wasn't exercising his prerogatives as king of the New Orleans brothels. But Morton frequently worked the backwoods barrelhouse circuit, like any other turn-of-the-century pianist who enjoyed eating regularly. Among the early barrelhouse pianists were a number as accomplished and versatile as Morton—Little Brother Montgomery, for example, was equally at home in a juke joint or a jazz band. Other barrelhouse men played little more than one blues in one key, but if they could rock the joint, they could be every bit as popular as their more musically literate brethren. In the work camps, sophistication and virtuosity counted for nothing. When Morton or Montgomery worked in such places, they banged as hard and rocked as singlemindedly as they were able, building their performances around the most basic and forceful blues riffs. In more relaxed, less dangerous surroundings, the more ambitious pianists worked on "test pieces" to challenge competitors. The most widely disseminated of these

Roosevelt Sykes

pieces, and the most rhythmically complex, was known generically as "the 44s." Each pianist personalized the piece with his own lyrics and instrumental flourishes, and soon after Blind Lemon Jefferson opened up the recording field for hard blues in 1926, a number of pianists recorded their "44" variants.

Little Brother Montgomery's "Vicksburg Blues No. 2" was perhaps the most rhythmically supple version, a record of great beauty that can still raise goosebumps today. The remarkable but little-known Lee Green learned it from Montgomery and passed it on to Helena-born pianist Roosevelt Sykes, who enjoyed a sizeable "race" hit with his own "Forty-Four Blues." The characteristic vocal melody became a favorite of guitar bluesmen in Mississippi and neighboring states, recorded by Robert Johnson as the razor-edged "If I Had Possession Over Judgement Day" and by Muddy Waters under its more familiar, generic title, "Rolling and Tumbling."

But Little Brother Montgomery, who apparently wrote the 44s or at least distilled it from oral sources, came closest to capturing the hair-trigger tensions of its inner polyrhythms on record. Montgomery played jazz, ragtime, and pop tunes with aplomb and knew exactly what he was doing with the 44s. He called it "the hardest blues in the world to play," explaining that it required the pianist to articulate "two different rhythms in each hand." The tricky syncopation of the vocal line further complicates the picture. Listening to Montgomery's "Vicksburg Blues No. 2," with its astonishing independence of left- and right-hand parts and the play and push-pull of rhythmic ambiguities in each hand, the listener keeps trying to decide which part, or implied part, cues the downbeat of each vocal phrase. But as in so much West African ensemble drumming, the one simple, repeating rhythmic figure that binds together the whole is never stated. It "isn't there," *except in the musician's mind.* By internalizing the central figure and syncopating each of the audible rhythm parts in fluid, shifting counterpoint to it, Montgomery performs a kind of rhythmic equivalent of sleight-of-hand.

It is in the imaginal realms of the 44s and other richly unorthodox barrelhouse staples that Professor Longhair's brand of sleight-of-hand, nurtured by both his barrelhouse gurus and the street rhythms of New Orleans, connects with the heart of the blues tradition. For the men Longhair chose as teachers were barrelhouse bluesmen one and all. Fess remembered one of them, Kid Stormy Weather, in particular because "he had strong hands, strong fingers, wrist, elbows, shoulder, and, uh, *movements* to what he'd do. He'd get the real soul of it." A Kid Stormy Weather who played piano on records by the Mississippi Jook Band, with a small recording group drawn from the Memphis Jug Band, and perhaps other artists,

Little Brother

Montgomery

on at least one mid-thirties recording session in Hattiesburg, Mississippi, may or may not be the teacher Longhair remembers, but his scrabbling rough-and-ready style makes him a likely candidate.

Another barrelhouse man Longhair learned from was one Rocky Sullivan, "but they all called him Sullivan Rock. He had the voice and the expressions a person really needs to fulfill what Stormy Weather wasn't puttin' in. Stormy Weather would give me the complete movements, the motions, but he didn't *sway* with 'em to make it feel like everybody could get into it. And Sullivan Rock was a fast man for octaves and jumps on the piano. I couldn't reach an octave then, my hands were too small, but Sullivan Rock started me to jumpin', and from jumpin' I had to come across other keys, and I learned what I call cross-chording to get the natural keys I want."

Although every blues pianist worth his salt developed his own distinctive bass patterns, two basic types can be identified in the recordings of the twenties, thirties, and forties. There was the driving, relentless boogie-type bass, which was called "fast western" early on because of its association with Texan and other Southwestern musicians; and there were the sparser, percussive, deliberately broken-up ostinato bass figures, which had roots in late-nineteenth-century Afro-Cuban music and in Cuban-flavored dances popular with North American blacks, such as the twenties "black bottom." The second type of bass, almost certainly the older of the two, was already being written out as a left-hand figure in ragtime sheet music in the 1890s, and it was this pattern, with its straight triplet bass and fluidly syncopated right-hand cross-rhythms, that Jelly Roll Morton referred to as the "Spanish tinge" in his music. Since identical bass patterns and counterrhythms can be heard in the earliest recordings of the Cuban *son*, and given New Orleans' status as a busy Caribbean port, the "Latin" bass is almost certainly Cuban in origin.

As the driving music of the barrelhouse pianists followed black migrations from the deep south into the big cities, it was taken up by polished musicians, who began turning it into a virtuoso performance music. Chicago pianists Albert Ammons and Meade Lux Lewis and Kansas City pianist Pete Johnson made such a powerful impression with their thundering volume and hell-for-leather, fast western-style basses that their appearances at John Hammond's *Spirituals to Swing* concerts in Carnegie Hall in 1938 and 1939 and their ensuing residence at New York's Cafe Society Downtown, sparked a nationwide boogie-woogie craze in the early and mid-forties. In a few short decades, rocking bass had moved from the barrelhouse to the pop mainstream—even the Andrews Sisters sang about their "Boogie Woogie Bugle Boy." But popular boogie pianists like Ammons and Lewis, who were a formative influence on Fats Domino, Amos Milburn, and other postwar players, were familiar with Afro-Cuban basses as well as the fast western style. In fact, Ammons's and Lewis's Chicago mentor, an older man named Jimmy Yancey, employed the "Spanish" basses almost exclusively. Later tributes by his students, such as Lewis's "Yancey Special," inevitably reflected the "Spanish tinge."

But the increasingly formulaic slickness of boogie-woogie as a popular entertainment hardly affected Deep South piano traditions. The Southern barrelhouse circuit continued to produce outstanding pure-blues pianists well into the forties and fifties, men like Johnny Jones (featured with Elmore James's Broomdusters) and the last of the great blues band pianists, Otis Spann. Both men were from the piney woods and knew the work-camp barrelhouse well.

And right at the center of these disparate but related piano blues traditions stands Professor Longhair. He played as forcefully and rocked as hard as the toughest of the barrelhouse pianists, yet his command of the nuances of Jelly Roll's "Spanish Tinge" was subtler, more rhythmically sophisticated than that of any other blues pianist of his generation. A stint in the Civilian Conservation Corps during the Depression further developed his rhythmic acuity. "I played with a lot of West Indians, Puerto Ricans, Jamaicans, Spanish boys, Hungarians," he recalled. "I just copied all their changes and beats and the ones I liked, I kept 'em." Hungarian? Well, Fess did call one of his early combos Professor Longhair and his Shuffling Hungarians. At any rate, he remembered "playing these things I'm playing now" as early as 1938–39. But it was not until 1949 that Professor Longhair began recording, and his career briefly took off and flew about as far as it was going to go.

By mid-1949, everyone in black New Orleans seemed to be talking about Professor Longhair. His scrappy little combo was actually competing with the popular, polished, musically literate jazz and jump band led by trumpeter Dave Bartholomew for choice local gigs. Record companies from the east and west coasts were beginning to visit New Orleans in search of talent, and Ahmet Ertegun, a founder of Atlantic Records, has given a vivid description of his first encounter with Fess on one such expedition. Having heard the legend and eagerly bought it, Ertegun and his companions were directed to a wooden juke house on the outskirts of town. Slogging through a farmer's field, splashing mud all over their New York sharpie suits, they could hear the noise of the joint from perhaps a mile away. As they approached, they saw that the place was more than packed; wild-eyed fans were

leaning precariously out the doors and windows, hollering and carrying on. And you could still hear the music over the din. According to Quint Davis, founder of the New Orleans Jazz and Heritage Festival and the man most responsible for reviving Fess's career, "Fess used to play piano with two microphones, one in the top and one in the bottom, in the body of the piano. He'd wear steel-tipped shoes and kick with his feet at the bottom of the piano where the second mike was. He used to kick a piano to pieces in a month—just destroyed them." To which Fess added, "It destroyed me too."

After their muddy ordeal, Ertegun and friends finally made it to the joint and squeezed inside. They must have looked ludicrously out of their element, but the music was some of the strongest and most abandoned they'd ever heard. During a break, they approached the wildman at the piano about recording for their then-fledgling Atlantic label. He said he'd be glad to. "Oh, by the way," he added, "I already made some records for Mercury." Ertegun and his associates thought they'd found a diamond in the rough, but Fess had actually recorded for Star Talent as well as for Mercury and was already experienced in the studio. Atlantic recorded him anyway.

Star Talent had recorded Fess in a New Orleans nightclub, and while the session features the first rendition on wax of his future standard "Go to the Mardi Gras," the sound is very muddy, the young players nervous sounding. (Incidentally, two of the four men in Longhair's 1949 combo became key New Orleans session players and R&B innovators a decade later—drummer John Boudreaux, who powered many of Allen Toussaint's early productions, and saxophonist Robert Parker, who had a classic R&B/proto-funk hit of his own with "Barefootin'.") But nobody sounds nervous on Fess's first Mercury session of August 19th, least of all Longhair himself. The slow-grinding, lubriciously swampy grooves are years ahead of their time, especially on "Byrd's Blues" and "Her Mind is Gone." The latter tune encapsulates everything that is original and off-the-wall about Fess's sense of humor. "Called her yesterday morning, she called me in the afternoon," he complains, "she said, wait a minute daddy, I was talkin' to the man in the moon / You know her mind is gone...." "Bald Head" ("Hey, looka there, she ain't got no hair") is more inspired lyric lunacy, this time set to an old whorehouse/tent show tune (New Orleans pianist Archibald later recorded a similar ditty).

Somehow, the lyrics' craziness and Longhair's unique foghorn voice were entirely of-a-piece. He was much more talented as a singer than he is customarily given credit for. His timing could be devastating, and whether he was communicating humor or heartbreak, he had one of the broadest vocabularies of tonal effects, rasps, honks, strangled cries, and sliding glissandos to be heard on any blues records of the period. For the doctrinaire blues purists, "Hey Now Baby" from the first Mercury session and the jumping "Between the Night and Day" from the second, not to mention "Willie Mae" and "In the Night" on Atlantic, should be sufficient to establish his blues credentials once and for all. These early sides also show that while he was a master at sliding back and forth between superimposed double- and triple-time feels and syncopating against those Cuban basses he also had a mean, driving left hand. The Mercury "Oh Well" has a ferocious boogie-style walking bass, and Longhair is able to vary the groove on other numbers from more or less straight boogie to a sideways-staggering, lopsided boogie to an almost ska-like shuffle.

Despite the success of his second Mercury session, which found him fronting an experienced studio rhythm section with the great jazz guitarist Walter "Papoose" Nelson, Fess often seemed to fare best with musicians he had trained himself. Boudreaux and Parker may have been overeager teenagers, but they stuck right with Fess' tricky syncopations. When Atlantic put Fess together with Dave Bartholomew's crack studio musicians in 1953, saxophonist Red Tyler, a thoroughly schooled bebopper, complained about Fess' "unorthodox" approach. There are a couple of instances on the Atlantic Longhair collection, *New Orleans Piano*, that feature acutely uncomfortable sax soloists sticking to the most basic and pedestrian 4/4 melodic statements while Fess's piano dances around them, double-timing and moving freely from three into four and back again. But while the Atlantics have been justifiably praised, it's the 1949 Mercury sides that really capture Fess in his prime the controlled but unrestrained vocals, the songs, and the grooves are superior, and it sounds like Fess is banging the living daylights out of the piano. There's a booming, low-register rumble to the piano sound on the Mercurys, probably deliberately minimized by Atlantic's tidy production.

The Mercury recordings leave little doubt that Fess would have been loud enough for any barrelhouse, with or without a band. The vocal inflections, bends, and slurs, and the sound of the piano (partly attack and touch, partly the willfully abrasive inner voicings of Fess' "alias keys") are the very essence of the blues. If the music's attitude seems today to be pure rock and roll, all swagger, lust, and jive talk non sequiturs, it's worth remembering that the same attitudes had been permeating blues for decades. Peetie Wheatstraw's thirties records primarily advertised what a bad-ass he was, Tampa Red wanted to "play with your poodle," and even Delta blues paradigm Robert Johnson crowed, "Stuff I got'll bust your brains out, baby, it'll make you *lose* your mind." Here Fess was one step ahead of Johnson; *his* woman's mind was already gone.

When the Mercury single "Bald Head" began looking like a hit, Longhair joined a tour that featured bandleader Dave Bartholomew and his new protege, Fats Domino. He returned to New Orleans vowing never to go on the road again, a decision that can't have helped his subsequent career. His recording during the fifties and sixties was sporadic, but with works of sheer genius scattered along the way. Any list would have to include the Atlantic "Tipitina" (the original single version on the Nighthawk LP *Mardi Gras in New Orleans*, not the inferior alternate take on Atlantic's own *New Orleans Piano* compilation). His 1957 Ebb sides "No Buts No Maybes" and "Baby Let Me Hold Your Hand" and the definitive 1959 Ron recording of "Go to the Mardi Gras" are equally essential. And "Big Chief," his mid-sixties collaboration with former Guitar Slim understudy Earl King, is one of the great New Orleans singles, whether you consider it blues or not.

During the early seventies, around the time his house burned down, Fess' constant companion was a small, taciturn man known only as Shiba. They shared two obsessions: gambling and music, specifically Fess's music. Their adventures as card sharps may never be known, but Fess and Shiba did record a remarkable session in 1971. Shiba's style was as individual as that of a Delta blues drummer like Peck Curtis or Willie Nix: never a hint of a backbeat or shuffle figure, just a barrage of accents that somehow fell in all the right places. If Shiba could read Fess's mind in a card game as well as he read it on the bandstand, the pair must have cleaned up.

But drummers could also be Professor Longhair's bane— when a conventional drummer sat in one night, I heard Fess complain that "I was up to sixteenth notes and tryin' to get up to thirty-seconds until that drummer come up and brought us down to a one-two-three-four." There were no such problems with either Shiba or Zig Modeliste; Longhair called Zig "the best man I've found so far. He's got a pair of hands *and* imagination."

The 1971 session with Shiba, and four tunes from a 1972 date with Zig Modeliste, are on Longhair's *Houseparty New Orleans Style: The Lost Sessions; 1971–72* (Rounder). These sessions were "lost" for so long because they were recorded quickly and intended as demos. But they were Fess's first studio outings after his rediscovery and return to performing, and he was champing at the bit. To me, *Houseparty* is the finest of Fess's postcomeback albums. In addition to its exuberance and intensity, and Longhair's rapport with both drummers, on this record he leans more toward "straight" blues—"Thank You Pretty Baby," "Gonna Leave This Town," "Every Day I Have the Blues," "Dr. Professor Longhair." *Crawfish Fiesta* (Alligator), released the day Fess died, on January 30th, 1980, is a fitting memorial, but *Houseparty* is the Longhair collection I'd take along to that desert island.

Like Muddy Waters, Fess died quietly in his sleep; they both just slipped away. A personal and almost preternaturally perfect sense of timing was central to both men's art, and apparently that sovereign sense of timing never deserted them. But I'd prefer to remember Fess as he was the last time I saw him, in New York City a few months before his death. He was fronting the tight, well-rehearsed band heard on *Crawfish Fiesta*; the dark, cavernous Village Gate was packed and jumping. Nobody was just sitting and listening; even the critics were up and dancing.

I remember pouring sweat on the dance floor, beginning to lose myself in the irresistible rhythmic undertow, when I noticed a florid, flushed face looming up into my face. It was Alan Lomax, the distinguished folklorist who'd recorded Son House and the pre-Chicago Muddy Waters and so many other American masters for the Library of Congress, but he wasn't acting distinguished that night. He was screaming. I couldn't catch what he was screaming over the music and the crowd, until I turned my "good" ear in his direction. "This music!" he roared. "This music we're hearing, *right here, right now*, is at this very moment the BEST GODDAMN MUSIC that anybody could POSSIBLY be making, anywhere on this planet. THIS MUSIC IS THE CENTER OF THE WHOLE GODDAMN UNIVERSE."

Allen Toussaint, one of an imposing list of acknowledged Longhair disciples that includes Huey "Piano" Smith, Dr. John, and many others, performed a medley of Fess's themes at the funeral. It was the sound of Fess transfigured, playing those same funky figurations but playing them the way an angel might. I was in tears, but then I remembered Lomax and had to smile a little. Surely one of the greatest miracles of this music is that it could lead anyone, even a folklorist or a critic, to drink deep from the wellsprings of Eternal Truth. Rave on, Professors Longhair and Lomax, rave on.

B.B. KING

FROM BEALE STREET
TO THE WORLD

by Pete Welding

Since the end of World War II, when electric
amplification of instruments gave the traditional blues of the southern countryside
an exciting new lease on life, tens of thousands of blues have been recorded by
literally thousands of performers. Most have languished in obscurity but a number
of these singers and instrumentalists have managed to achieve notable success,
commercial as well as artistic, performing and recording extensively, influencing
other performers, enriching and leaving their own stamps on the musical traditions
from which they have sprung and to the advancement of which they have contributed.
Few, however, have had anything approaching the sustained impact and success of
B. B. King. In a professional career now entering its fourth decade, the singer-guitarist
has seen the blues style he developed in the late forties and early fifties become the
universally dominating sound of the modern blues and he, as its architect and
incontestably its single finest representative, one of the most important figures in
all of blues history.

King's accomplishments and their significance are staggering by whatever criteria one chooses to assess them. In terms of purely personal achievement, he has become the single most popular and successful of all blues performers, with more top-selling blues and R&B recordings to his credit than any other performer of modern times, and has enjoyed in recent years a conspicuous degree of success in the wider arena of general pop music. He has been, in fact, one of the few performers to have gained this type of broad acceptance while continuing to remain fundamentally a performer of blues and like music. While King occasionally has attempted nonblues material—not just in recent years but in the earlier stages of his long career as well and largely, one suspects, at the urging of his record producers—the real foundation of his music, no less than his great success, has been the direct, earthy fundamentalism of the blues which he continues to perform with a brilliant, fervent contemporaneity of feeling as have few others.

King's feeling for the music is one of deep, unfeigned affection. "For us [black Americans], the blues is almost sacred," he has noted. "Like Gospel music. Because it's a part of our culture, and a part of us." The key to the blues' enduring appeal is simple, he explained: "As long as you've got black people, there'll always be blues," and as for himself, King states proudly, "I don't class myself other than just a blues singer. "

While his success as "just a blues singer" has been great indeed, measurable by such things as hit recordings, sustained record sales, a busy performing schedule at top venues, music poll awards, and like testimonials of popularity and achievement, the extent of King's accomplishment goes far beyond such immediately tangible manifestations into the very fabric of the modern blues itself. The true measure of his success is taken by the fact that King's music, born of his vision and then painstakingly worried into perfection over years of hard, meticulous work, has shaped and colored the whole of the modern blues to the degree that virtually no performer of the music since his time has escaped the pull of its all-pervasive influence. So powerful, richly expressive, and, above all, hugely popular has been King's special handling of the blues that few in fact have wished to do so, and in one way or another every blues performer of the last quarter-century has been his heir, student, or offspring. To test the validity of this observation, one merely has to listen to the recordings of the younger, post–B. B. King generation of blues artists. Not only is his stamp everywhere present in their singing and playing but, more significant still, there has been no major stylistic development in the music since his appearance that is in any way comparable to his.

There can be little doubt that King's has been the most absorbing, widely imitated of all blues approaches brought forward in the modern (i.e., post–World War II) period of the music's development, the one that most tellingly has communicated the actual, ongoing contemporary experience of most black Americans over the last thirty years. While other postwar blues approaches found favor with various, largely localized black audiences—in particular those of Chicago, which satisfied large numbers of newly urbanized Southern blacks who shared common backgrounds with blues performers from the same region—most such musical styles enjoyed relatively brief periods and limited degrees of success. The tempo of modern life was much too quick, its experiences too complex, and its rate of change much too rapid to be mirrored, for very long at least, by approaches so firmly rooted in the black past. Which is why, I think, the blues of Muddy Waters, Howlin' Wolf, Elmore James, John Lee Hooker, and other postwar performers from the Lower South, for all the strength and frequent beauty of expression they achieved in their music, failed to sustain beyond their initial years of popular acceptance. The musical impulses at the core of these approaches were too rigidly anchored to the country blues of the agrarian South to reflect much more than a transitory, early stage of the modern black experience.

On the other hand, King's approach, which utilized quite a different mix of influences than those which operated on their music, has had a much more universal appeal and a longer-lasting impact. While it was shaped at much the same time as were the postwar Chicago blues, his particular synthesis of traditional blues, jump band music, swing, and, to a degree, jazz and mainstream popular music has proven much more widely and enduringly expressive of postwar black culture. It more faithfully mirrored the actual experiences, thoughts, and preoccupations of most black Americans, as well as according better with their emerging self-identity in a period of broad, rapid cultural change; as such it was much more immediately satisfyingly responsive to their needs than was the more fundamentally rural-centered music of the Chicago bluesmen.

It is well known that social change is reflected, often with surprising rapidity, in a society's cultural expressions—in the folkways, music, art, language, and other manifestations of the creative spirit to which the culture gives rise. It is not so much that the artist initiates change as that through his heightened sensitivity to such tendencies already at work within his culture he comes to early awareness of them and, if he is sufficiently adept in handling his art's traditional expressive forms, articulates these new ideas in ways that are pleasing and meaningful to his contemporaries. In doing so he reduces the threat that often accompanies change in traditional, conservative societies, thereby facilitating the process of assimilation by which such change is harmoniously integrated into the culture. While this mediatory role is only one of a number of functions through which the folk artist serves his community, it assumes great importance during those stressful periods when change must be accommodated.

The success a traditional artist, such as the blues performer, enjoys when his culture is going through a process of sustained, rapid change—such as has characterized, for black Americans, the entire period since World War II—is a direct result of how successfully his art has reconciled, with their often opposing tendencies, its past, present and, to a degree, its immediate future. Some performers, Waters, Wolf, James, and Hooker among them, were able to evolve approaches that, for a time at least, effected a helpful reconciliation of past and present but were unable to incorporate into their music a vision of the future sufficiently informed or comprehensive to permit it more than a temporary acceptance. For this reason, their success was relatively short-lived. With its relentless, ruthless sweep of change, time simply passed them by, and from the mid-fifties on their music decreasingly addressed in any meaningful way black listeners. (Fortunately for them, a number of these and like country-based blues performers were enabled to continue with their professional careers when, beginning in the early sixties, their "discovery" by young white folk music fans opened a sizable new audience for their music.)

B. B. King suffered no such decline either in listenership or in popularity, for his music was, to use an overburdened but applicable word, more immediately relevant to larger numbers of blacks, and for a much longer period of time, than were the early postwar blues styles of Waters, Wolf, and like country-cum-city traditionalists. This does not mean, of course, that King's was "better" or more artistically satisfying music than theirs, but merely that in a number of important, far-reaching ways it was different, and significantly so. To communicate effectively in the postwar period the blues performer had to evolve a different handling of the music's traditional forms and means if he was to successfully embody in his music the vast, rapid shifts in world view, lifestyle, self-image, values, aspirations, and all the other large and small matters brought about by the radically different pressures of modern urban life on the black American. As time has borne witness, King's music was able to do this better, more fully and satisfyingly than any other single approach devised for the blues in the postwar period.

To understand why this was so, one must examine the man, his life, music, and, in particular, the various lines of influence that came

B. B. King and his first

wife, Martha.

(facing page)

together in the formation of his musical style and which set it apart from those of other postwar blues performers. It must be remembered that, like Waters, Wolf, Hooker, and a large number of other early postwar blues artists, King was a native Mississippian, born Riley B. King on September 16, 1925, on a plantation located midway between Indianola and Itta Bena in the northwestern part of the state, about 125 miles south of Memphis. A generation younger than those performers, King's childhood and early adolescence was not much different than theirs had been, and largely was spent in farm labor—milking cows, ploughing, hoeing, and picking cotton, and the like. His parents had separated when he was four, and King's mother, taking him with her, moved to a community farther east in the hilly part of the state, where the youngster remained for the next ten years.

From the age of nine when his mother died, King was on his own, although he continued to live with and work for the white farming family that had employed her. He recalled that he received $15.00 per month as a farm laborer, working long hours through most of the week, attending school when he could, and walking a total of ten miles each day to reach the one-room schoolhouse in which he received such elementary schooling as he did. At the time, he related later, he was not aware of experiencing hardship.

"Now, believe me," he told writer Stanley Dance, "it was one of the happiest parts of my life because there, then, they were just simple people.... I had a mule and a plough when I was twelve, and we used to plough six months out of the year. On the plantation, we always worked five-and-a-half days a week, usually six, and often six and a half. I once tried to figure out how far I must have traveled in ten years of ploughing, six of them behind a mule. I never heard of a vacation until I left the plantation. Kids work in the South when they are not at school. We would go to school in December and January, when it was cold, but when it stopped raining we would begin working. They plant the cotton in the middle of March and when it comes up in April the kids have to start hoeing. They lay it by when it is stronger than grass, and it opens around October 5th.

"I was a very good cottonpicker," the singer recalled. "I've picked almost 500 pounds of cotton in a day, which is a lot of cotton. I was really a very good farmhand I'm proud to say. I remember that nowadays whenever I have a big hit, remember when I earned 35 cents for picking a hundred pounds of cotton. A good cottonpicker would usually work from around nine in the morning to six in the afternoon."

After a separation of ten years, King's father located him and brought the youngster to his home in the Delta area, near where he had been born fourteen years earlier. At first, King said, he chafed at the loss of independence this move entailed, for he had largely been his own master for nearly five years, but he soon adjusted to the new life and family in which he found himself, his father having remarried and had several children by his new wife.

Then too, it was at this point that King discovered music. One of his aunts was married to a Sanctified minister, Archie Fair, who also played guitar for church services. The youngster was drawn to the instrument and began to teach himself to play whenever he had access to it, usually on Sunday afternoons when, following morning church services, the family members would gather at one or another's homes to eat and socialize. King liked the instrument so much that he soon had made arrangements to acquire a guitar of his own, which he obtained from a friend at a cost of eight dollars, his employer taking the money in small installments from his wages. At first he confined himself to performing religious music, much of which he learned from his preacher-uncle.

"That was how my musical career began," he told Dance, "but there were no teachers of music through there that I ever heard about. Four of us boys got a little quartet together, but I wasn't interested in blues then. I always thought I might be able to get somewhere in the spiritual field. The Golden Gate Quartet were our idols, and we'd hear them on the radio. I learned by just watching and listening to that preacher play. I kept fooling with the guitar and I learned three chords. It seemed though I could sing almost anything with those three chords, like 1, 4 and 5."

Despite his fondness for spirituals and other religious music to which he had gravitated because of having been raised in what he described as "a spiritual type of background," King was exposed to the recordings of some of the great early blues performers. "About the time when I started playing guitar," he recalled, "I had a young aunt who was just like the teenagers of today—you know, buying all the popular records. And that's how I heard blues people like Blind Lemon Jefferson, Lonnie Johnson and Robert Johnson. Out of her record collection, Blind Lemon came to be one of the guys who would stay with me all the time."

In addition to this introduction to blues, King recalled meeting various local and visiting performers from whom he learned additional guitar technique. "I began to run into different guys who were playing guitar," he reported,

"and I'd ask them things. I met Robert 'Junior' Lockwood and Sonny Boy Williamson, and it was Sonny Boy who later gave me my first break. The work scene was fairly plentiful. They'd play the plantation halls and joints where a lot of gambling went on. The men who ran them would hire any name that would bring the people in. Those that danced went into the dancehall part, and those that wanted to gamble went in the other. A guy who could draw could easily get a guarantee of two or three hundred dollars, because the man who had the joint could probably make that much at the door, plus his gambling. Sometimes they'd have a trio, and sometimes it might be Sonny Boy alone—and you'd be surprised how they'd dance to just him and his harmonica.

"A lot of times, when guys like Sonny Boy came to Indianola, I wouldn't have any money, but I'd try to slip in. I'd have to walk there, and we lived eight miles out of town. You might be lucky enough to get a ride *to* town, but you'd have to walk back that night. Johnny Jones had a nightclub there, and he was really the guy who kept the Negro neighborhood alive by steadily bringing people in, like Louis Jordan, who was real popular during this period, around 1939. So was Charles Brown. Johnny Jones was a very nice fellow, and he knew the guys on the plantations didn't have any money during the week, but he would often let us in and we would pay him off when we came in Saturday."

W.C. Handy, 1930.

When World War II commenced King was inducted into the army but, following training at Camp Shelby and a brief stay at Fort Benning, Georgia, was sent back to Mississippi, where he spent the duration of his military service as a tractor driver on a large farming plantation. "It was a funny thing," he observed, "but it was when I went into the army that I started singing blues. A lot of fellows seemed to get religious and sing spirituals when they got in there, but me, I didn't. When I got home I realized a lot of fellows were making a living singing the blues, but my people were very religious and I was afraid to sing the blues around the house. My aunt . . . would get angry with anyone singing the blues, I would have to do that away from the house, but I found later on that people seemed to like my singing and playing."

It was during the war years that King was introduced to the recordings of several instrumentalists whose styles were to exert strong influences on the shaping of his own approach to blues guitar. Among these were several jazz performers. "I heard Charlie Christian," King recalled, "and this is when I began to get kind of acquainted with jazz. This is when he was with Benny Goodman. And at the same time, I used to listen to Jimmy Rushing and he was with Count Basie. So you see the link? By listening to them, I began to get interested in big bands.

"Then a buddy of mine, who was in France, heard Django Reinhardt and he brought back some records with him. So Django became an idol of mine, along with Blind Lemon, Lonnie Johnson, Charlie Christian—and, oh yeah, I remember one Saturday night when I came to town—you know, after you worked all week on the plantation, Saturday night was our little bit of outlet—I heard an electric guitar that *wasn't* playing spirituals. It was T-Bone Walker doing 'Stormy Monday,' and that was the prettiest sound I think I ever heard in my life. That's what *really* started me to want to play the blues. And of course I was crazy about Oscar Moore, and then I heard Johnny Moore and that did it!"

It was about this time that King began to perform in public, although in deference to his relatives' feelings about blues singing, he chose not to perform in the immediate area but traveled to adjacent towns in the Mississippi countryside. "I would work all the week and sometimes on a Saturday I would have eight or ten dollars," he recalled. "I would take this money and buy me a ticket to the nearest little town, me and the guitar. I would go to this little town and stand on the corners and play. The people seemed to like it and they would tip me a nickel, a dime, or a quarter. That sort of thing is still done in the South. Sometimes on a Saturday I'd visit three or four towns, sometimes as far away as 40 miles from where I lived, and sometimes I'd come home with maybe 25 or 30 dollars. So I found I made more in that one day than I had in the whole week. The money was nice, but that wasn't all of it to me. I wanted to do it, and it made me feel good that they enjoyed listening to me."

King followed this practice for several years immediately following the end of the war, his skills continually growing as his confidence in his abilities to entertain listeners deepened. Finally, he felt he was ready to test himself on the busy musical scene of Memphis. Every important musician of the Lower South had gravitated to this city since the early days of the century and, as a result, it supported a large, competitive musical activity in which virtually every black musical style could be heard. In 1947 King, with a friend, hitchhiked from Indianola to Memphis, where he soon found employment and located, as well, his cousin Bukka White.

One of the great rural blues performers, White was sixteen years older than King and already had made a number of recordings in classic Mississippi Delta blues style. He made his first records for Victor in 1930, when he was only twenty, and seven years later recorded several titles for Vocalion, one of which, "Shake 'Em On Down," became something of a hit, and soon proved one of the music's standard, much-recorded pieces. Following this, White was sentenced to a term of imprisonment at Mississippi's Parchman Farm, during which he recorded two titles for a Library of Congress field recording team headed by folklorist John A. Lomax. On his release from the prison farm, the singer-guitarist undertook a marvelous session of twelve titles for Vocalion in March of 1940. On some of this session he was accompanied by Washboard Sam, but most of it found the singer underscoring and punctuating his dark, deeply emotional singing and highly personal lyrics with powerfully percussive, antiphonal guitar work of great drive, complexity, and sensitivity. These performances remain among the great landmark recordings of the country blues.

The two men began spending time together, the young performer learning a great deal from the older man. King described White as one of his major influences, adding, "The older people know him, just as they know Big Maceo, Tampa Red, and Leroy Carr. A lot of the singers who were based in Chicago toured the South, because that was where the best audience was. The blues-minded people were mostly those who were born and raised down there. They did more for the artist than the northern cities. These people brought their ideas of how it should be, and usually their records, when they came north. Then, too, guys like Blind Lemon came to Chicago, but they would usually go back.

"Bukka was a lot older than me, and he used to record. He had a steel bar he would put on his finger, and the sound he'd get from the strings with it would go all through me. I never could do that, but I learned to trill my hand, and with the help of the amplifier I could sustain a tone. Sounds are more important to me than trying to play a lot of notes. It's like automobiles. You can have speed or economy, not both."

Years later King described the impact Memphis made on him, a young man newly arrived from the country. "Beale Street isn't what it used to be," he said, "and it was really Beale *Avenue*, not Beale Street. It's about a quarter-mile long, ten or twelve blocks, from the River to the East. I remember when Handy's Park used to be like a circus. Beale Street runs along its south side, Third Street on the west, and Hernando on the east. There used to be parties, jug bands, and everything going on there, something in each corner, but the crowd usually ended up with the blues singers. It wasn't like a theater with the names up outside. There you had to be heard, and whenever a fellow got to feeling good, there all the people would go. But it got to be so noisy that the all-white police ran the cats out. They were attracting so much attention that they were tying up traffic on Third Street, which is a main thoroughfare. They still tried, and some days good policemen would let them carry on a while. Another park they used to settle in was Church Park, in the Negro part [of town].

"When I came there, Beale Street had already changed some, and there weren't so many places to play as they claim there used to be. They still had some of the familiar places like the One Minute Cafe, where winos and people like that could get a coke and a hotdog for a dime when they got hungry. Or they could get a nickel's worth of chili, and stuff like that. Then they had two or three theaters, but it wasn't like it was in Handy's day, which I've heard about from oldtimers, when there were many, many clubs, where you could go and gamble and everything.... Memphis seemed nice to me, and a big change coming from Mississippi, just as it was later going to Chicago and New York. But Memphis is a nice place to live. It's called 'The Gateway to the South' because all the main highways leading to the South come through the city, and there's a famous bridge across the Mississippi River there."

King's next move was to try to establish himself on the city's musical scene. He was assisted in this by singer-harmonica player Rice Miller, who, using the professional name "Sonny Boy Williamson" as he had for several years (creating confusion with the "original Sonny Boy," John Lee Williamson, a native

Tennessean who until Miller's appearance had been the foremost blues harmonica player and a greatly popular recording artist; he died in Chicago in 1948), was then broadcasting regularly on radio station KWEM in West Memphis, Arkansas. Hearing Miller-Williamson's daily shows, King determined to seek him out. It was his hope that the older performer would be able to steer some work his way.

"Sonny Boy Williamson had a radio show every day in West Memphis, right across the river in Arkansas," King recalled. "So one day I went over there. He had Robert 'Junior' Lockwood playing guitar with him, Willie Love playing piano, and a drummer. This was the second Sonny Boy, the one whose biggest record was 'Eyesight to the Blind,' and not the original Sonny Boy who made the Bluebird records. He was about twenty-five years older than me, and maybe even older than the original Sonny Boy.

"They remembered me from Indianola and I asked him if he'd let me do a song. He said yes, but he'd have to hear it before they put it on the air over this station, KWEM. He liked it, put it on the air, and told the people to call up if they liked it. And they did. Fate had it that he had two jobs this particular night, so then he said, 'Look, boy, I've got a job, and if the lady will take you, I'm going to let you play it while I work somewhere else. And you better *play* or you're going to answer to me!'

Magic Sam forged

an immediately

identifiable style that

would not have

been possible without

B. B. King.

"He called the lady and she said okay. The 16th Street Grill was one of those joints I was talking about, with dancing, and gambling on the side. Gambling was legal. It was wide open there, and sometimes the sheriff or the police would come by. It was the same on the plantations, but there the boss man would only call the sheriff if someone got hurt real bad, and on some of those plantations there would be a thousand families. Well, the lady agreed to pay me twelve dollars a night, five nights a week, and my room and board. She said I could keep the job if I got on the radio daily. This was more money than I'd ever had before in my life."

In insisting as a condition of his performing in her club that King secure radio exposure, his prospective employer was simply following a practice that had become prevalent in the late forties. It was believed that regular radio broadcasts would create great interest in a performer's club or dance engagements; he, moreover, was expected to liberally "plug" these appearances during his broadcasts, thus ensuring a large attendance. A number of performers in the Lower South followed this practice, Williamson and Howlin' Wolf among them, using their regular radio broadcasts to build followings for their music, bolstering their record sales (if they happened to have recording contracts), as well as advertising upcoming engagements. It was a sensible procedure, for black listeners followed such shows avidly, black music having then only recently begun to be featured at all extensively on southern radio stations. King was fortunate in securing a ten-minute midafternoon show, sponsored by the makers of Pepticon, a health tonic, on WDIA, a Memphis station that had just made the switch to an all-black programing policy following its earlier activities in white country music.

"They didn't pay me," King recalled of this early show, "but I could advertise where I was playing, and that was my objective in the first place. After that, they would bring me on every day as the 'Pepticon Boy,' and later this got so big that they had to give me more time." The radio exposure was of great benefit to King; the show proved so popular that not only was his airtime expanded but he was able to assemble a regular group of his own to perform at the various engagements that started coming his way. The broadcasts had created a demand for his music and, while he earned little from his radio work, he more than made up for it in the fees he earned from his performances.

"I got me a little trio with Johnny Ace on piano and Earl Forrest on drums," the singer recalled, "and on the two nights I had off from the lady's place I would go out and do one-nighters. Even before I got the trio, I could earn twenty-five dollars by myself. I didn't know what to do with all this money, and I messed it up. I started drinking and gambling a little bit. Guys would give me [hard luck] stories too, and I was very generous. I don't regret that.

"When one of the disc jockeys left the station, they made a disc jockey out of me, and they said I'd have to get a new name. The product that sponsored me was selling so well, and I was on the air for them fifteen minutes a day for about fifty dollars a week. It got so popular that on the Saturdays the salesmen would take me to the little towns outside Memphis, and we'd have a big truckload of the stuff, and I'd sit there singing, and they'd get rid of any amount of this tonic that was supposed to be good for tired blood. One of the salesmen said they would listen to me because they could see I had an honest face!

"The first name they gave me on the station was 'The Boy from Beale Street,' then it got to be 'The Beale Street Blues Boy.' The people got hip and started calling me 'B. B.,' and that was how the name B. B. King came about. I did very well and got very popular, so when another disc jockey left they gave me his show too, and I ended up with two hours and 15 minutes a day. I used to sing along with the records once in a while, and record companies that put out blues began to get interested. I was still doing one-nighters with the trio around the city, sometimes a hundred miles away, but never so far away that I couldn't be back in Memphis by morning."

In 1949, less than two years after his arrival in Memphis, King made his first records—four titles, "Miss Martha King," "When Your Baby Packs Up and Goes," "Got the Blues," and "Take A Swing with Me"—for Bullet Records, a

B. B. King, age 20.

(facing page)

small Nashville firm that went out of business soon afterward. Whatever their performance strengths or weaknesses, the recordings were notable for their use of a small horn section along with the more usual rhythm-section backing of piano (played, incidentally, by the young Phineas Newborn, who was later to achieve fame as a jazz keyboard virtuoso), bass, and drums. The use of horns, which has been an important adjunct of King's approach to blues throughout his career, is a direct result of his longstanding admiration of such popular black entertainers as Louis Jordan, whose exuberant "jump-band" fusion of blues, jazz, and popular music had deeply impressed the young performer a decade earlier. King's interest in this approach to music had steadily deepened as his involvement with blues had increased over the following years. Too, his growing fondness for jazz, and especially the large Swing orchestras of Count Basie, Duke Ellington, and others, had opened his mind to the possibilities of annealing certain of its instrumental procedures, colors, and effects with those of the standard small-group approach to blues.

Moreover, King's several years' experience as a disc jockey had exposed him to large numbers of recordings in the then emerging West Coast blues style, many of which supported their featured vocalists with small horn ensembles, a legacy of this music's earlier grounding in the jazz-based, horn-accompanied music of the Texas-Oklahoma region from which many of the West Coast blues performers originally hailed. Additional incentive came from the great popularity during the late forties of blues instrumental records, many by saxophonists, in the early days of what was then called "blues and rhythm" music. As a disc jockey active during this period of hectic musical experimentation, King heard the recordings of Wild Bill Moore, Big Jay McNeely, Hal Singer, Jimmy Forrest, Paul Williams, and other popular jazz-cum-blues instrumentalists. He learned from all of them.

"Whereas most bluesmen have been content to work within a narrow stylistic scope," wrote Barret Hansen of King's music, "deriving their styles almost exclusively from other bluesmen, B. B. became a true blues eclectic. He combined an enormous number of musical elements, inside and outside the blues idiom, to form a style which was radically different from anything that had gone before, yet so true and natural that within a year or two after he made his first records B. B. was renowned across black America as the 'King of the Blues.' "

More than anything else, what distinguished King's approach was its knowingly balanced incorporation of these diverse elements with those of the traditional blues of his rural Southern upbringing. While many shared with him this common background, King was one of the first blues performers to draw extensively on the wide, richly varied world of music opened to him by the phonograph record. Through recordings the young performer had been exposed to a much broader spectrum of musical influences and had, as a result, access to a wider musical palette than was available to older performers from the same area as he hailed from. Being a generation older than King, blues performers such as Muddy Waters, John Lee Hooker, Howlin' Wolf, and Elmore James, for example, had been exposed to no such musical diversity. Coming of age in the late twenties and early thirties as they did they were limited, by cultural no less than geographic isolation, to the musical styles of their immediate localities, to which occasionally were added influences from visiting performers or from blues recordings from outside areas, many of which differed little from the favored local styles.

The phonograph record, radio, motion pictures, and other media, among other forces, changed all this and as the thirties and forties advanced a large number of musical-cultural traditions were disseminated ever more widely. It is King's achievement that while his earliest musical education was little different than that of virtually every other blues performer of the Lower South, he later expanded this through his fascination with, and study of, a number of musical idioms previously felt to be outside the scope of traditional blues. The use of horns in section, deriving from his love of orchestral jazz, was one of these. Gospel music, one of his earliest musical experiences, was of course another, and this influence is most evident in his freely expressive approach to singing, generally more melodic in character and rich in the use of melisma, falsetto, and other techniques associated with gospel singing and in consequence remarkably free of the cadential, more narrow melodic compass of country blues.

However, what most markedly differentiated King's music from that of his contemporaries was the brilliant guitar style he had fashioned from a number of sources and which was increasingly showcased on the marvelous recordings he undertook, beginning in 1949, for the Los Angeles–based RPM Records, one of the more successful of the so-called "independent" record operations started during the war years.

Developing from the relatively simple religious music and country blues he had learned as a youngster in the Mississippi countryside, King gradually had extended and refined his guitar technique through the forties, his early emulation of the styles of Bukka White, Elmore James, Robert Lockwood, and like country bluesmen gradually giving way to more advanced techniques learned from the recordings of Lonnie Johnson, Blind Lemon Jefferson, Robert Johnson, and other adventurous, innovative players. The next major influence he absorbed was that of T-Bone Walker, the Texas-born singer-guitarist whose groundbreaking, highly exciting approach of extended linear improvisation and broadened, jazz-based harmony, played with powerful, imaginative fluency on amplified guitar, soon became the chief basis of King's own approach.

King has frequently acknowledged the great impact Walker's music made on him, and credits the older man with developing the modern blues guitar style. "T-Bone Walker," King has noted, "had a touch that nobody has been able to duplicate.... I've tried my best to get that sound, especially in the late forties and early fifties. I came pretty close but never quite got it. I can still hear T-Bone in my mind today, from that first record I heard, 'Stormy Monday,' around '43 or '44. He was the first electric guitar player I heard on record. He made me so that I knew I just *had* to go out and get an electric guitar."

In assimilating Walker's style into his own, King gradually smoothed out the older man's aggressively staccato attack into one of greater subtlety, emphasizing a more relaxed legato handling of line that much more closely approximated that of his singing, using the guitar in fact as a responsive extension of his voice. This was a process that required several years to bring about, and on his earliest RPM recordings, dating from 1949 and 1950, one may hear a guitar style still in its formative stages, with King more often than not performing with a harder, more aggressive attack and a harsher tonal quality than has characterized his more familiar mature approach. The style is in fact quite close to that of his model without, however, being an outright copy of Walker's. "You see," King explained, "I used to try my best to play like Lonnie Johnson and T-Bone Walker, and I could never really make it. My fingers just wouldn't do it. Say I had stupid fingers. But if I could have copied them I would have. Instead, I guess I just got ideas from them."

Then too, there was King's professed admiration of the jazz guitar approaches of Charlie Christian, Django Reinhardt, Oscar and Johnny Moore, Bill Jennings (guitarist with Louis Jordan's Tympani Five), and Les Paul. His fascination with their music undoubtedly played a not-inconsiderable part in the shaping of the guitar style he introduced on his first recordings for RPM, although much of his knowledge of the fundamentals of these approaches was rudimentary and largely, one suspects, instinctual. At this stage of his musical development he was self-taught and as a result had too limited an understanding of the fundamentals of music to come to a truly informed appreciation of their efforts. Still, he absorbed what he could grasp, adding it to his arsenal of instrumental effects.

On more than one occasion King has noted that the approach toward which he was working so determinedly during the late forties and early fifties derived in large measure from his appreciation of a number of jazz soloists whose work he admired—Christian, Reinhardt, Jordan, Cootie Williams, and Lester Young (whose note-bending on saxophone he sought to emulate on guitar) among them. Within the context of a familiar, clearly defined blues framework King wanted, and worked consistently to attain, the improvisational freedom of a jazz soloist. It is to his great credit that he eventually achieved his goal, for blues, and all American music, has been the richer for his having done so.

There was, too, King says, a practical reason for his having concentrated on the development of a guitar style that, like Walker's, was built around the use of single-string runs as a responsive, answering voice to his singing. "From the very beginning," he recalled, "when I first started playing, my coordination wasn't very good, so trying to sing and play at the same time didn't get to me. I'll put it this way: while I'm entertaining, while I'm trying to get my breath, or think of a new line to tell you, then the guitar takes over, until I think of what I'm going to do. If I'm singing, then I have to hit a chord and hold it, because I could never try to sing and play to myself at the same time—now, I could hit on the guitar, but I'm talking about making sense with it. "

In addition to providing King the nucleus of his guitar approach, T-Bone Walker's influential recordings of the forties also furnished him an idea of the proper use of horns in a blues framework. "T-Bone used to use a lot of horns—trumpet, alto, tenor, and baritone," the singer recalled. "They made a beautiful sound, like shouting in the Sanctified churches, in just the right places. He had a good rhythm section too. And to me T-Bone seemed to lay right in between there somewhere. That was the best sound I ever heard."

It was in this area, incidentally, that King initially experienced some difficulty. While he wanted to use horns in a context that would "make sense" with his blues singing and playing, his record producers felt, and rightly so, that his earliest efforts in this direction were improperly focused. King himself concurred in this opinion, noting that in those days, "you couldn't get anybody who could play blues the way they wanted it, but then I began to run into guys who are now very big in the jazz field, like George Coleman, who [later] was with Miles Davis. Herman Green, who was with Lionel Hampton, was with me for a time, and so was George Joyner, the bassist. I got Phineas Newborn his first union card, and he, his brother Calvin, who plays guitar, and his old man,

B. B. King

(facing page)

who plays drums, were all on my first record date. Booker Little, and fellows like that, worked with me, too.

"We worked together, but they didn't always like it, because my timing was so bad. My beat was all right—I'd keep that—but I might play 13 or 14 bars on a 12-bar blues! Counting the bars—that was out! These guys would hate that, because they had studied, but all my musical knowledge was what I'd got from records. I tried to play it right, but I ended up playing it my way. The one thing they did like was that I paid well. I could afford to pay them twenty or twenty-five dollars, and if I made more, I paid more. They liked that so much that they would be running to get the job, even if they hated what happened to the bars. There wasn't that much work then, and by my being on the radio so much it made mine the most popular band in the city. Another reason those musicians liked working for me was because they could go out, be back, and go to school next morning. I was a young man myself then, about twenty-two."

Aside from a certain amount of stridency in his handling of the instrument and a lack of originality and cohesiveness in the use of horns, the difficulties King reported he had been experiencing in these areas—at least with his working band—were not reflected in his recordings of the period, which remain among the finest blues records of the late forties and early fifties. Following his recordings for Bullet, King in 1949 had signed a recording contract with RPM Records and it was with this Los Angeles–based firm (which maintained for some years a Memphis office) that he enjoyed his first commercial success. "I made eight or nine records," he recalled of his first several years with the label, "and some of them sold pretty good. They weren't hits, but the company made money on them. Then I came up with one of Lowell Fulson's old tunes which I'd always admired—'Three O'Clock Blues.' I did that in 1950 and it climbed on top of the R&B charts in 1951, and it stayed Number One for eighteen weeks."

The record immediately established King with the blues audience, and its success led, as well, to representation with a top booking agency, lucrative touring, and engagements at the leading R&B venues, nightclubs, and concert halls. It also enabled the singer-guitarist to assemble and keep together a first-rate orchestra of seasoned professionals with which he performed regularly (his booking agency had insisted on this, in fact), leading inevitably to the solution of many of the musical problems that earlier had plagued him. A proper orchestral format having been settled on, King was then freed to concentrate on the perfection of the guitar style toward which he had been working, and from the early fifties on his playing

Otis Rush, another

offshoot of the

B. B. King school of

guitar playing

who styled a distinctive

and searing

sound of his own.

(facing page)

increasingly took on the original, distinctive character so long identified with him and which has become universally known, admired, and emulated as the foremost modern blues approach. (King never has stopped working on the development of his music and, like many topflight instrumentalists, constantly strives to improve and refine aspects of his technique, at one time working toward greater control of tone projection, at others toward speed and execution, and so on, in a never-ending quest for mastery of his instrument. Likewise, he has continued his studies of theory and harmony, in which connection he took up some years ago an intensive study of the system of musical composition and related theoretical matters devised by Joseph Schillinger.)

For all its benefits to King's career and musical development, "Three O'Clock Blues" was merely the first of many top-selling recordings he was to have through the fifties. These included "You Know I Love You" and "Story from My Heart and Soul" in 1952; "Woke Up This Morning," "Please Love Me," and "Please Hurry Home" in 1953; "You Upset Me" and "Whole Lotta Love," a double-sided hit from 1954; "Everyday I Have the Blues" and "Sneakin' Around," another double-sided hit, and "Ten Long Years" in 1955; "Crying Won't Help You," "Bad Luck" and its discmate "Sweet Little Angel" (the first and third of these deriving from earlier recordings by Robert Nighthawk, the slide guitarist being one of King's acknowledged favorites), and "On My Word of Honor," all dating from 1956; the twin hit "Troubles, Troubles, Troubles" and "I Want to Get Married" from the following year; and "You've Been An Angel" and "Please Accept My Love" from 1958, during which year, incidentally, the RPM label was discontinued, King's subsequent recordings for the firm appearing on the new Kent label.

The performer's string of hits continued through the sixties and into the seventies. During 1960 he had, in fact, four top-selling records on the charts, "Sweet Sixteen," "Got A Right to Love My Baby," "Partin' Time," and "Walkin' Dr. Bill," and scored twice the following year, his final year with Kent, with "Someday" and "Peace of Mind." It was in this year, 1961, that he switched to ABC Records on the termination of his Kent contract. One of the chief reasons for this move, King explained, was his dissatisfaction with Kent's practice of releasing his recordings, including many of his hits, on the budget-priced Crown Records label the firm operated for a time in the late fifties and early sixties, the LPs bearing a retail price of $1.98 and frequently selling for considerably less than that. Such a price, however attractive to the consumer, did not provide the singer much in the way of royalty-derived income from his record sales.

King, however, continued to have hit after hit for Kent throughout the ensuing decade. He had recorded extensively during the nearly dozen years he was with RPM-Kent and after his departure the firm released many of these older recordings, often scoring R&B success with them. Ironically, most of King's numerous hit recordings through the greater part of the decade, up until 1968 in fact, were with his old Kent masters—"My Sometimes Baby" and "Gonna Miss You Around Here" in 1962; "Blue Shadows" in 1965; "Eyesight to the Blind" and "I Stay in the Mood" in 1966; "It's a Mean World" and "The Jungle" in 1967; and "The Woman I Love" in 1968. Additional Kent hits were "Worried Life" in 1970 and "That Evil Child" in the following year, ten years after his ceasing to record for the firm, tribute to the continuing relevance, power, and appeal of his distinctive approach to the blues.

In 1966 he had his first hit for ABC with "Don't Answer the Door," one of his top-selling records, and over the following years he has had many more for ABC and its companion BluesWay label: "Paying the Cost To Be the Boss," "I'm Gonna Do What They Do to Me," and "You Put It on Me" in 1968; "Why I Sing the Blues," "I Want You So Bad," "Get Off My Back Woman," and "Just A Little Love" in 1969; "The Thrill Is Gone," "So Excited," "Hummingbird," and "Chains and Things" in 1970; "Ask Me No Questions," "Help the Poor," "Ghetto Woman," and "Ain't Nobody Home" in 1971; a remake of "Sweet Sixteen," "I Got Some Help I Don't Need," and "Guess Who" in 1972; "To Know You Is to Love You" and "I Like to Live the Love" in 1973; and "Who Are You" and "Philadelphia" in 1974.

B. B. King

(facing page)

It was during this latter period that King made a breakthrough into the wider area of general pop music, and virtually every one of his successful recordings since the groundbreaking "The Thrill Is Gone" of 1970 (produced with taste and discernment by Bill Szymczyk) has placed in both the R&B and the general pop music charts of topselling records. While a few others have been enabled to capitalize on his success in this area, their music as a result enjoying wider audience acceptance, King remains the uncontested leader in the move to the blues-drenched "crossover" musical style that has proved so vastly popular with listeners, black and white, during the seventies. Thanks to his continuing receptivity to, and unfeigned interest in, a wide variety of musical idioms—"from Bach to B. B." is the way he described his listening habits—he was able to make the transition to this more expansive approach more easily and naturally, with greater interpretive authenticity and emotional conviction, than have any of his contemporaries or followers. Where King led, in fact, they have followed, as has been the case for the last quarter-century.

"I like to be original," King has stated. "I always like to have something new, and if other guys like it well enough to copy, then I try to get something else. I continue to study every chance I get, but I come back to the *sound*. I still haven't got the sound I actually want, but I think I'm pretty close to it.

"My ambition is to be one of the greatest blues singers there have ever been. I've had a lot of things in my favor. I'm trying my best to get people who don't like the blues not to hate them. You may not like something, but you can still respect it. Maybe I'm defending what I'm doing, but when I stand on the stage and sing and sing, and people don't understand what I'm doing, I almost cry.... The blues are almost sacred to some people, but others don't understand, and when I can't make them understand, it makes me feel bad, because they mean so much to me."

CHESTER BURNETT:
THE MAN WHO BECAME THE WOLF

by Ed Ward

The sun was going down over West Memphis, the red glow in the air maybe the heat of the sidewalks being released. He sat on the porch, watching it, sipping from a paper cup. Only coffee in this cup tonight, he told himself. Keep a clear head for the drive. Five hundred something miles, but I ought to be able to do it in a day. Get out on the highway, just open her up, keep an eye out for the highway man.

Once that coffee was gone, that was the last of West Memphis. Drink it down, throw that cup far from the porch so it doesn't so much as touch the car. He'd beat the dust from the seat of his pants and brush off his shoes before he took off, too. Don't want a bit of this place following me to where I'm going.

Not that West Memphis was a terrible place. It had done its duty by him: he'd come to town in dungarees with bust-out knees and those shoes that never fit, so he'd worn down their backs. And here he was leaving in a 1952 Cadillac he'd paid $4,000 cash for, with another $3,900 in his pocket. He'd made all of that, and lots more

that had gone to rent and food and good times, right here in West Memphis. What was it that song said? Life begins at forty? He'd been thirty-seven when he'd come to town, and he was forty-two now. Guess so, except things were about to get a whole lot better if he had anything to say about it.

What was sad was that his boys didn't see why he was doing it. He'd told them over and over, come on up to Chicago with me: y'all are my band, you played on my records—well, except for 'Struction, who didn't show up, so it was lucky that skinny Ike Turner knew how to play the piano—but he'd told them, I'm the one who's takin' the risk: if the people don't like my music, this money of mine ain't gonna last long, and this Cadillac be up on blocks or up for sale, and y'all be gone playing with anybody you want. Chicago got a lot of singers, they need guitar players, they need drummers, and every bar got a piano. And we got a record contract with Mr. Chess. But they just shook their heads. Plain country.

But he knew that it wouldn't be that way, whether they came or not. It was a matter of knowing you were right. He knew he was right when he came to town, and that Cadillac parked there was the proof. When he'd been on the radio, he'd known that all the people liked his shows, even if it had led to that white boy getting angry and getting him fired. And now he knew he was doing the right thing, going to live in the same city as his record company, as his fans—or at least the new ones who'd bought his record and put it right up there in the Negro top ten.

Man, he figured the drive would take about twenty-four hours. Get up there, sack out for a couple of hours, change into the clean, pressed suit he had packed, and go out on the prowl. Let Chicago know that the king was on the scene. The Howlin' Wolf had arrived. Find some poor tired guy fronting a band and go in there and destroy him. Go for blood. The mighty Wolf! Damn, he was getting jacked up from the coffee. Time to hit the road. And when he had a place to live, he'd send for Lily and the boy.

He forgot to dust off the seat of his pants. He didn't brush his shoes. The dirt would settle deep into the car's upholstery and carpeting, and wherever he drove it, the dirt would go, too.

We don't know much about Howlin' Wolf. We don't know exactly where he was born—although it was somewhere in Mississippi—or, really, when, although June, 1910, is what people usually say. Thanks to dedicated researchers, most notably Pete Welding, we can follow young Chester Arthur Burnett —yes, named after the president—as his family farmed in one place, then another. We know he got his first guitar when he was eighteen, and that he wasn't particularly good or bad at it. He sang in a church choir as a young man, and what a sound that must have been! But it didn't take him long to realize that singing by himself, with the guitar and the harmonica, was the way to go.

His model for this was Charlie Patton, one of the Mississippi Delta's most idiosyncratic bluesmen. Tall, thin, with wavy hair (Patton claimed Indian and Puerto Rican blood), he'd started his career in the Delta, but between living off women and getting paid for performing, Patton soon became an itinerant performer, following the crops and the money. He gave the people their money's worth, too: he'd use his guitar as a percussion instrument, play it behind his head, with his teeth, or as he thrashed around on the ground on his back. In 1928, when Chester was eighteen, Patton had been staying around the plantation the Burnetts were working, so Chester, having just gotten his guitar, boldly approached the older man and asked him for lessons. Patton showed him a few licks, and tried to teach him his "Stone Poney Blues," his biggest hit. Chester didn't learn it completely right, but he did it okay, good enough to start daydreaming about all the extra money he'd earn on weekends once he really learned.

He also learned harmonica, just so he'd have another instrument, and here, too, he managed to find exactly the right teacher. He was a guy named "Rice," who had a thing for Chester's half sister and later wound up marrying her. Chester would wait for him to come over and get comfortable with the girl, then he'd come into the room and demand to be taught something on the harmonica. To get rid of him, Rice would show him a thing or two, and then tell him to get lost until he could play what he'd just shown him. Chester never got quite as good as Rice, who later took the name Sonny Boy Williamson from a Chicago bluesman who'd just been murdered, but he did well enough. Eventually, he and Rice wound up on the road with another Delta legend, Robert Johnson, but that didn't last long. Johnson and Chester were about the same age, and Rice was ten years older. Johnson was a much more experienced traveler than the other two, always eager to go somewhere else, and it wouldn't be surprising to learn that, if he even bothered to ask them to come along, neither Chester nor Rice had the self-confidence to do so at this point.

Howlin' Wolf with Hubert Sumlin on guitar at Sylvio's, Chicago.

(following overleaf)

Chester was a big boy, and he got bigger. All his life, he had trouble with shoes: his feet were sixteen inches long. People around called him Bull Calf, or, unsurprisingly, Big Foot or Foot. But that wasn't the name he wanted to use when he played. Just as his brother-in-law was to do later, Chester Burnett stole his performing name from a lesser bluesman named J. T. "Funny Paper" (or "Funny Papa") Smith, a guy whose gimmick was playing a guitar-banjo. Smith called himself "The Howling Wolf," but Chester knew the name was properly his, so he took it.

Daylight always did something to his sleep, even after all these years. Without actually waking him, it made patterns of warmth on his body, and played across his closed eyelids, bringing forth images. He'd hit the sack at about 3:30, so that the sunrise caught him at that period of sleep when the mind is deep inside. The paper shade helped, but not much, and only most of the adrenaline he'd whipped up to get on the stage and go into his act before a disbelieving crowd had been pissed off with the beer.

They'd called him Grandad, although Chester had no idea if the man was really his grandfather. He was old, no doubt about that, and his memory went back, not only to slavery days, but to Africa. He loved to smoke those pipes he carved as he sat in his chair in the shade, and he loved to talk to the kids. Chester had been about eight, sitting there shucking corn for his mama and listening to the old man go on. He had good stories about animals, about the lion, the king of the jungle, whose mighty roar could be heard for miles around as he proclaimed a kill. "But you ain't got no lions over here, boy," he said. "Up in the mountains you got some cats, but they ain't much. Come down, steal your chickens maybe, but a fox'll do that. No, they ain't much. I tell you what's the king around here, that's your wolf. Ain't too many of 'em left: they scared people too bad. See, they smart, like a dog, but they got the killer left in 'em, which a dog mostly don't have. And they smart. You can catch one as a pup and raise it, you got better'n a dog, but they'll run off, they will, and they won't recognize you if they see you later. But that's contrary to nature, turning a wolf into a dog. He don't want that. He'd rather you meet him halfway. Oh, yes! You know there's mens'll turn into wolfs. Don't look at me, boy! I seen it. The hair come out on 'em, they stoop down and walk on four legs—yes they do!—and they run into the woods and run with they brothers all night long. And howl? Oh, the noise they make: Aeuuuuuu! Ahooooo! Aeuuuuu! They say 'Can't you hear me cryin'?' 'cause they scared they might not turn back when the daylight come." "Do that again, Grandad." "Huh? You mean that wolf cry? Aw, I can't do it like those mens that've got changed. Aeuuuu! Naw, that ain't it. Anyway, that don't hardly happen these days. Like I said, the people's killed the wolf off, and without a pack to run with, don't nobody change. Can't: wolf runs in a pack. A lone wolf, now that's somethin' to reckon with. He either real smart or real crazy if he ain't runnin' with a pack, and if he crazy, you don't want to be around. Naw, you don't want to mess with a lone wolf; it just ain't smart."

So he'd lay awake at night, listening for the sound without knowing what he was listening for. The woods bordering the plantation were scary. He'd been chased once by a wild hog, with tushes and everything, and he knew there were deer, little ones that came out to the edge of the field as the sun was going down. There could be anything in there, and he just knew there were wolves. He was also sure that somebody on this plantation ran with them. He'd seen men creeping out at night. Maybe that's where they were going.

Then, about six months later, some men had dumped a furry corpse in the dust. Chester crept up to look at it. "Is that a dog?" he asked, hoping the answer would be yes. The men laughed. "Boy, ain't you never seen a black wolf before? That's no dog, that's a black wolf." His eyes had filled with tears and he'd run off into the fields, and everybody assumed it was because he hadn't liked being kidded by the men. But they'd shot a lone wolf, and without really thinking of why, it had rushed on him like a tragedy. It upset him so much that he never credited the true story of Lonnie, who'd disappeared one day, just like that. Just up and gone one night. Lonnie had caught a ride on a cotton truck and was living with his cousin in Memphis, but you'd never have convinced Chester of that, not after he'd seen the dead wolf.

The unfamiliar sunlight and the image of the furred, bleeding thing jolted him toward wakefulness. He turned over and got up to piss. Back in bed, he drifted off toward sleep. "The mighty wolf has come to your town," he'd sung at the crowds in the joints he'd gone to last night. A lone wolf. Real smart or real crazy?

Chester Burnett may have sized himself up before a full-length mirror in a dry goods store one day when he went to town, and thought about his career. He wasn't a particularly distinguished guitarist, and although he was okay as a harmonica player, he wasn't a patch on Rice Miller. He weighed 275 pounds, so he wasn't a skinny, handsome man like Charlie Patton or Robert Johnson, and his head was, like the rest of him, big and square. On the plus side, though, he sure did love playing blues.

The compromise was simple: he had a wife (although she was to die young), and he knew farming. He would farm for his father, but if and when he could scare up a chance to play somewhere in the area on a weekend—which, because the plantation owners wanted as much labor as they could get from their tenants, was the only time opportunities like that presented themselves in the country—he'd take it. It was easy money: you only had to play for twelve hours, and you got paid as much as you'd make on the farm all week long! Plus, unlike chopping cotton, it was fun work, work accompanied by fried fish sandwiches, soda pop, beer, or rotgut red whiskey, and amorous looks from daring young women—which could get you killed: it had Robert Johnson. You could even do the work sitting down: the Wolf preferred to sit when he sang, although he'd spend a good part of the show stalking around, or flailing around on the ground in the throes of theatrical lust, or even crawling on all fours.

So Chester spent his twenties working with his father, farming around northern Mississippi, and taking off from time to time to perform at rural dances. Occasionally, he and his father would head up to Memphis, where they saw jug bands performing on Beale Street. The idea of a band really appealed to Chester: for a long time his favorite musicians had been the Mississippi Sheiks, which his neighbors the Chatmons had put together, and had had a lot of success with once they started making records. But given what he was making performing, the idea of getting a band together was ridiculous. Anyway, he kept reminding himself, he was a farmer.

That is, until he became a soldier. Considering his size, it's amazing that the Army would want PFC Chester A. Burnett, but they took him in 1941, and he spent the war doing something or other around Seattle. He never spoke about this period of his life, although, to be fair, he never spoke about his life much at all. But it's probably safe to say that the Wolf didn't howl much in Washington State.

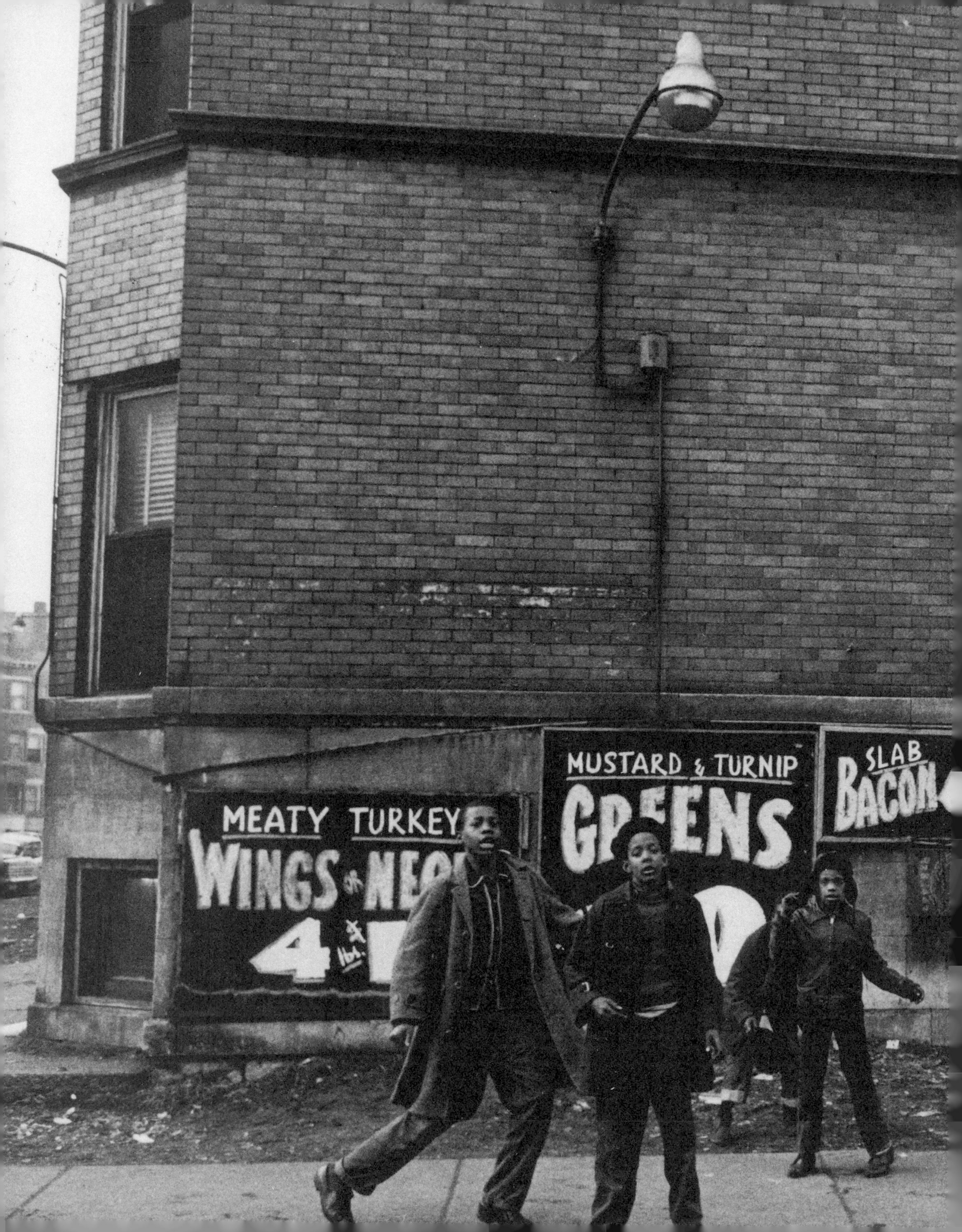
MEATY TURKEY
WINGS
MUSTARD & TURNIP
GREENS
SLAB
BACON

After leaving the Army, Chester moved back with his father "until I figured I was grown enough to go by myself," as he told Pete Welding —a very strange thing for such a self-assured man to say about himself at the age of 35. But Chester left his father, finally, and farmed for two years in Penton, Mississippi, a town that doesn't show up on my map of the state and may have vanished. "I made two crops there," he told Welding, "and then I moved to West Memphis, Arkansas."

Behind this laconic statement there lies, in all likelihood, a titanic struggle in the soul of Chester Burnett, a wrestling match between Chester and the Wolf. Chester was thirty-eight, a married man (he'd remarried to a woman named Lily who would bear him a son and three daughters), and even if he wasn't particularly brilliant as a farmer, at least it was something he'd been doing his whole life. He wasn't going to move to West Memphis to farm, needless to say. It was the backside of Memphis, Tennessee, like East Saint Louis is to Saint Louis, the part of town where people went to sin. It had a corrupt municipal government, and a load of speakeasies, whorehouses, and bars. Memphis had Beale Street, which was, in relative comparison to West Memphis, genteel. The colored aristocracy came to play on Beale Street. West Memphis was something else entirely.

No, Chester wasn't going there to farm. He was going there to give in to the thing that was disturbing his sleep, that wouldn't let him farm in peace. He was going there to become the Howlin' Wolf.

It happened fast. Almost immediately, the Wolf had a band, young kids of eighteen, nineteen, and twenty years old: Willie Johnson on guitar, Willie Steele on drums, and William Johnson on piano. It was easy keeping the two Willie Johnsons separate: the way the one of them played the piano, everybody just called him "Destruction." Sometimes M. T. "Matt" Murphy would be there on guitar, and all manner of harmonica players, like Junior Parker and James Cotton, would sit in: there were a *lot* of harmonica players in Memphis in those days.

The Wolf was canny, and he did two smart things. First off, he almost never played Memphis, preferring to keep the band over in West Memphis and make his reputation there instead. The second move was that he approached KWM, the local radio station, about a job, and got a deejay slot that started each afternoon at 3:00. He sold his own advertising, and spun records that he knew other country folk come to the city like himself would like. It wasn't this new, jazz-tinged blues: it was country blues, pure and simple, with the addition of electric instruments. Oh, sure, it sounded primitive, but it had the feeling that the country people liked, and it was the music that he and his boys played, too.

And so, just a couple of years later, Wolf and his band were approached about making a record. It made sense: the Memphis area was a longtime magnet for black musicians of all types, and after the war, independent record labels were springing up everywhere. Some, like the Bihari brothers' operations, Modern and RPM, which were based in L.A., even had talent scouts and a studio in Memphis where they could record the hottest thing going and get it out before the competition.

The Biharis' man in Memphis was Sam Phillips, who'd assembled his Memphis Recording Service out of bits and pieces of electronics and what he remembered from his days doing radio work in the army. Sam would record people as a sort of "record your voice" service, and when he figured he had something hot, he'd send it off. Or Ike Turner, a young guitarist who had been touring in an act called the Kings of Rhythm with his wife, Bonnie, would bring people into the studio to record. Ike was from East Saint Louis, and knew how to look at a scene and find its hot center, and in West Memphis, that hot center was Howlin' Wolf.

In July of 1951 Ike set up Wolf's band at Sam Phillips's place and recorded two songs, "Moanin' at Midnight" and "How Many More Years," and Sam Phillips went and sent the master tapes off to Chess Records in Chicago, for reasons that are too complicated to go into here and involve a flurry of lawsuits between the Biharis and Phillips. Ike did an end run around Sam and rerecorded the Wolf in somebody's living room with portable equipment, something he'd already done with B. B. King. He sent his master tape to the Biharis and called it "Morning at Midnight." Both records were released in September, 1951, and both hit the charts, although they ate up each other's sales, and neither had a distinct advantage. But Chess had something RPM didn't: "How Many More Years." Released in November, it shimmied right up the charts and broadcast the Wolf's fame far and wide.

The lawsuits were settled shortly afterward, and Chess wound up with the rights to the music Wolf recorded for Sam Phillips. Throughout 1952 he went back and recorded more, but the Chess brothers kept urging Wolf to move to Chicago, where he could find steady work in the clubs and the finest musicians around, who would be more than glad to record with him in Chess's up-to-the-minute recording studios at 2520 South Michigan Avenue. Finally, a few

Howlin' Wolf

(facing page)

weeks before Christmas of 1952, Wolf gave in. He'd already had to give up the job at KWM because the white deejay there was jealous of his popularity and the amount of advertising he sold, and so he turned over the farm he'd inherited from his grandfather to his brother in law, bought a Cadillac, withdrew his money from the bank, and drove off to Chicago.

One goddam thing Mississippi never had was snow. Having to wear a hat and an overcoat wasn't so bad, but the shoes hurt. You couldn't go barefoot in a Chicago February. So your damn feet hurt all the time, and you had to take care about wearin' a scarf, too, so your throat wouldn't get infected. Especially the way he sang, that was important. Of course, he had his tricks: he loved to watch "Howlin Wolf Junior" fools blow their voices out trying to imitate him. Nothin' succeeds like success. And he'd had some success.

Course, it was a trade-off, just like trading off the Mississippi warmth for the Chicago cold. Just like trading off the plantation where they grew the cotton for the one where they made the records. He was gettin' robbed, there was no doubt about that. It's just that it was too hard to prove it, especially with his schooling. He'd tried to bring it up to Mr. Leonard once, and all he'd say is "Muddy's happy."

Well shit, of course Muddy was happy. Muddy was their pet, thought he was the damn king of Chicago. Muddy'd come straight off the plantation and up to Chicago, without even stopping to get some city smarts the way he had, and he thought he ran the damn place. He'd been on Chess first, he'd been sellin' records longer, and he had a lock on the best musicians. They'd recorded with him, of course, but when he'd asked them to play the clubs with him, to go on tour with him, they got scared. "No, man," they'd say. "We Muddy's band." And Muddy was a cold motherfucker, too. It was obvious that Chicago suited his ass because he had cold Lake Michigan water in his veins. Didn't never have the time of day for the Wolf, cut him dead, couldn't even be civil. Too good to live, that Muddy Waters.

Well, to hell with him, because even though his run had lasted longer, he wasn't sellin' no records these days neither. He was down to havin' to tour, even go Tom to the white folks, go play a flattop guitar because they didn't think electricity

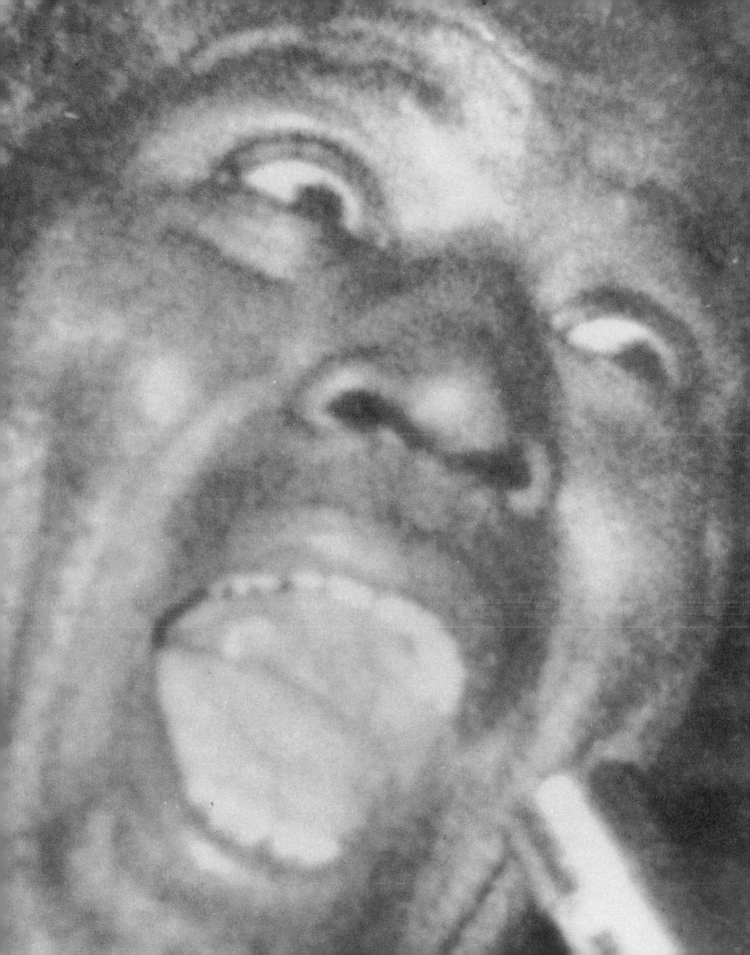

and blues mixed. It wasn't folk music. Shit, his last big record had been folk music: "Smokestack Lightnin'," a tune he'd heard way back before he'd even gotten his first guitar. And it was funny, because those kids in England knew what he was talking about, what his music was about, even if they couldn't play it worth a shit. What was it Rice had said after he'd gone over there and stayed a while? "Those kids in England want to play the blues so bad, and you know, they do play the blues so bad!" Rice, man. Whiskey finally got him last year. Little boy with a derby on.

And to hell with Muddy's band, too. They too good to play with him, he had a way around that, too. He'd taken the Cadillac back down to West Memphis, gone with Little Walter, who played with Muddy but was a star his own self, and he'd gone back to see his band, who weren't doing shit, working those same bitty places in West Memphis. And here come Wolf with Little Walter. Cotton, man, Cotton had gone nuts: his idol was there in the Wolf's car. They'd gone out to his brother-in-law's land, all dressed up nice, and had their picture taken, picking some cotton in their fancy city clothes. He'd come back in the car with Willie Johnson and Hubert Sumlin, double guitar dynamite. He was glad to have Hubert: he was good, and he liked to tell people he was his son. He wasn't, of course, but he'd part raised him, because Hubert was a little different, and his parents didn't understand him. You had to keep an eye on Hubert, but he could play guitar like nobody else at all.

Fact, Hubert had all but saved the Wolf's ass. Really, he hadn't hit on nothin' much after "How Many More Years," although a couple of his records, like "Evil," had done okay. Mr. Leonard had sat him down and told him his music was too country, that he had to make a change or else he'd have to let him go. "Blues isn't doing as well as it did a few years ago, Wolf," he said. He ought to know, sitting in there ripping off that light-skinned boy from Saint Louis, Chuck Berry, who was making him rich the way Wolf had made him rich (Muddy too, come to that). Well, the Wolf didn't play no rock and roll, but Hubert, bless him, had come up with a new way of playing his guitar. He'd let Willie Johnson go, and kept Hubert, and he'd gotten younger guys to play with him, Jerome Arnold, S. P. Leary, and after he left, Sammy Lay. It was a modern blues beat, and the people loved it just fine.

He turned on to Lake Street. Thank god for Sylvio's, he thought, that there was still someplace for him to play blues. And good thing they was friendly to those white kids who'd come in, too: he didn't think too much of them, but at least they paid their admission and bought his records, and he'd submit to some of their stupid question-and-answer sessions from time to time if they didn't get too insistent on pinning him down. What the fuck good did it do anybody to know exactly where he farmed in the thirties? Who cared about Robert Johnson? He's dead! No, he's really dead: he hadn't seen him laid out in his coffin, but people had said he was dead, and you didn't have to see some poor fucker stiff and cold like that to know he was dead, for god's sakes.

God damn. He was getting angry. And when he got angry, he got evil. And when he got evil, the people would just have to put up with it, because he was the Wolf, goddammit!

Tell you how simple those white folks are. One of them asked him why he'd stopped farming and started playing for a living. "I was good" is what he'd said. "Because I was good." You'd think somebody could understand that, couldn't you? Cold, but here's the club. And Hubert took his coat like a good boy and helped him onto the stage.

What little we do know about Howlin' Wolf really thins out once he got to Chicago. We know he made periodic trips back to his land to make sure his brother-in-law was taking good care, and we know that he toured a lot and sold a lot of records for Chess. He made records in which Mississippi was palpably present, cryptic songs whose stories seem to only be half there, like "Killing Floor," or whose imagery only makes sense in the most surrealistic way: what, after all, *is* smokestack lightning?

An older man—five years older than Muddy Waters, with whom he feuded nearly all his life—in the next-to-last generation of Chicago bluesmen, he had to work constantly to keep even with the younger men who were vying for the diminishing black audience with him. He never trusted white people much after he got to Chicago—not that he likely trusted them too much before then —and in 1970, he began protracted litigation with Chess's music-publishing wing, Arc Music, alleging that they'd cheated him out of royalties and had conspired to keep their foreign licensees from paying him royalties at all. In this, he had at least one thing in common with Chuck Berry.

In the early seventies, Wolf began to have heart attacks, and in 1973, still touring, he was in an automobile accident that pitched him through the windshield of the car he was riding in, which, in turn, started a series

of kidney problems from which he never really recovered. He kept on, performing from a chair, until the very end, mysterious, dark, and quintessentially the Wolf. He died in a veterans' hospital on January 10, 1976, while being operated on for an aneurysm. His funeral was held January 16 at the A. R. Leak Funeral Chapel, and according to the funeral program, he left his wife, Lily, two daughters, Mrs. Bettye Kelly and Mrs. Barbara Johnson, and two sons, Floyd Lee Burnett and Hubert Sumlin, one granddaughter, Kenya La Shawn Kelly, his mother, Mrs. Gertrude Burnett, a brother, four sisters, three aunties, nieces, nephews, and "an abundance of relatives and friends."

I'm one of those Howlin' Wolf left behind. As a folkie, my interest was piqued by blues, and, as I started college, I realized that blues was still being played in Chicago, that people like Muddy Waters and Wolf and so on were still making records. The Paul Butterfield Blues Band, who really opened my ears to Chicago blues, in fact, had Wolf's old rhythm section of Jerome Arnold and Sam Lay.

John Lee Hooker

(facing page)

One snowy morning as 1966 was just getting underway, a friend and I were in New Brunswick, New Jersey, for some reason that I've since forgotten, and we were driving around in what seemed to be a black neighborhood. I spotted a sign that said Blue Note Record Shop, and begged him to stop, which was okay with him. He immediately asked the lady behind the counter for James Brown records and I became certain she was going to throw us out. "Well," I said timidly, "do you have anything by Howlin' Wolf?" She looked at me like I was an idiot. "Of *course* I got the Wolf," she said. "This is a blues record shop, ain't it?" So I bought "Don't Laugh At Me," which I think had "Built for Comfort" on the other side, and I bought the *Real Folk Blues* albums by Sonny Boy Williamson (Rice Miller) and Wolf. This sort of initiation into this music made it very difficult, subsequently, to listen to white guys with long hair who were painfully sincere but woefully inadequate—when they were even that good—and made it completely impossible, a little while later, to listen to the likes of Ten Years After and the other groups who confused speed with soulfulness. It also made it impossible for me to warm to most of the modern black blues artists, who, I felt, were pitching their act toward the white college kids for whom they played. They had to, I realized, because black people in Chicago didn't listen to blues any more (the sort of blues that was still popular down South was smoother, with more soul music in it), but that didn't mean I had to like it.

Another thing: history made Chester Burnett Howlin' Wolf as much as Chester Burnett did. The historical forces that made him what he was can never be repeated, nor would any of us wish to see them repeated. But that also means that the product of those historical forces—the music he made, in short—cannot be duplicated. All we can hope for (and, at the moment of writing, it looks hopeful that this will come to pass) is that the people who now own the Chess legacy will soon present us with a coherent and well-thought-out collection of his works, similar to the ones of Muddy Waters's and Willie Dixon's they've put out in recent years.

We should also realize that the same historical forces that made Burnett's Wolf great made him a man nobody understood, a man many feared. A lone wolf is something to treat with a great deal of circumspection, and Wolf was a lone wolf for his entire life, despite those he left behind.

But he had to do what he did. He had to: he was good.

SOUL MAMA

by David Ritz

Under a full moon, Etta James stalks the stage. She wears no shoes, no socks. Her wavy hair is bleached blond. In a blousey black top and tight black pants, she makes no attempt to hide her obesity. Defiant about her size, she moves freely, gracefully. At fifty-two, her come-hither smile and smooth light-skinned complexion have her looking thirty-two. There's a mischievous turn to her mouth, a lascivious gleam in her eyes, a look-you-in-the-face-stare-you-down effrontery in the first words she sings:

"Your mama cooked a chicken, she thought it was a duck, she put it on the table with its legs cocked up ... I love you, baby."

Now she's off, deep into Jimmy Reed's "Baby, What You Want Me To Do," the thunderous beat of a restless black nation shaking the ground beneath her.

Her voice is the force of history, the extravagance of her emotions enough to encompass a whole people. She's a growler, a squaller, a church shouter who, as a child, bolted the congregation to sing whatever the hell she wanted to sing. Her aim is to shock the soul—your soul, her soul—to pull from the bottom of her vast musical body essential truths about pain and jubilation, loneliness and anger, fear and frivolity, unabashed sexual celebration.

Like the archetypal female blues singers who precede her by three decades—Bessie Smith, Ma Rainey, Alberta Hunter—James stands as a rebel, a front-line feminist in attitude if not in word, a woman strong enough to dramatize the outrage of her gender, to break the chains, tenacious in her power to put over the message and sing, "I don't want no watchdog ... I want a man."

Concurrently, Etta plays the victim, the brutalized woman, the willing codependent.

"He beats on me ... he cheats on me ... he's mean to me ... but he can be so sweet to me ... I'm gonna take what he's got."

Either way, sex is no secret. Etta turns to her audience, spreads her legs, gyrates her hips, licks her lips. The next morning the outraged jazz critic for the big-city newspaper will call her show a series of "vulgarisms." He'll be right—but only in the sense that Geoffrey Chaucer was vulgar. She's Everywoman's poet, an uncommon commoner, a humorist, a free spirit acclaiming the ribald, reveling in the pleasures of sensuous rhythm. Miss James is the blues—old blues, new blues, and all blues in between.

In 1955, when Etta James recorded her first hit, she was seventeen years old. A product of the fifties, that nascent decade when teenagers—teenage artists and teenage fans—were taking over, her vocal strength easily equaled her male contemporaries. The record which brought her fame, in fact, was a spunky reply to a man, to Hank Ballard's "Work With Me Annie." "Roll With Me Henry" (aka "Wallflower")—the Georgia Gibbs copy was sanitized as "Dance With Me Henry"—introduced Etta to the rhythm-and-blues audience, her mainstay for the next four decades. Her first deal was with Modern, the Bihari Brothers's seminal L.A. label dominated by traditional bluesmen turned electric— John Lee Hooker, Pee Wee Crayton, Elmore James, B. B. King. Her first mentor was Johnny Otis—soul orchestrator/composer/talent scout/entrepreneur extraordinaire— who discovered her at the Fillmore in San Francisco where she was performing with Peaches, a female trio. The group would dissolve, but Peaches, Etta's alter ego nickname, would prevail.

"When I saw Etta's talent," Otis tells you on his funky country estate in the foothills of Pasadena, "I was knocked out. She was a bolt of lightning, a thunderstorm, a tornado. She had the energy and she had the feeling. But she was a teenager and I told her, I said, 'Etta, I'll need your mother's permission.' 'Sure thing, Mr. Otis,' she said, and immediately got on the phone and had this long amicable conversation. 'Mama says it's fine,' said Etta, putting down the receiver. 'Mama says I can go.' I knew she'd been talking to the dial tone, but I went along. Etta's irresistible."

Etta's sitting alone in the dressing room, mopping her brow. The show's over and, together with the audience, she's drained. Her public self is spent. Her private side is shy, but there's something about you she trusts, something which allows her to speak candidly.

Her mind is quick; words runs in torrents, images and ideas sometimes colliding. Her voice is deep, resonant, heavy with reflection, light with self-irony. The product of rehabilitation programs and psychoanalysis, her language is a heady mixture of street locution and sophisticated self-understanding. You feel repercussions of the wars she's waged against herself; you sense her searching, seeking something lost long ago.

"I was born Jamesetta Hawkins in 1938 in Los Angeles. Now my mother was not a hooker—far from it—but my aunt did own a house on Twenty-fourth and Central, the Queen Elizabeth Apartments, and white boys would love to come by, and I do believe that's how my natural father met my mother. She was fourteen when he stumbled in. For six months another man was kept in jail for raping mama, but his skin was dark, not light like mine, and finally he was let go. The charges were false.

"Now me and Mama, we've always had an intense relationship, maybe the most intense of my life. We're close enough in age to make things interesting. It's interesting, too, that Mama loves music, loves it with all her heart, and the first music in my life was Billie Holiday, Mama's favorite. To Mama, Lady Day was the sun and the moon and all the precious stars in the heavens above. She worshipped Lady, and I did too. I appreciated the hurting Billie put on a song, the way she sang like a jazz horn. I knew she was a stone genius and I knew, too, that if I was going to sing, Mama would want me to sound like Billie.

Jimmy Reed

"But I didn't. And I don't. Fact is, I was drawn to the music Mama considered lowdown and beneath her. I loved funky blues. Don't ask me why. Just did. At an early age, I was into Guitar Slim. He sang "The Things That I Used to Do (Lord, I Won't Do No More)." Well, I'd put that sucker on our little Victrola and crank it up—all the way up—and I'd be grinding with the wall and Mama would be shouting, 'Girl, you ain't listening to nothing but trash.'

"Wouldn't matter what Mama said, because I knew what I felt. The music, the blues, the gutbucket thing was all up in me. I knew it had to come out. That was my spirit, my drive, my heartbeat. Man, it was my joy. Mama might have understood it, but never approved. To this very day, she's never come to see me sing.

"She also never mentioned my real father until I was eighteen. One day she called me from my bedroom to where she was watching television. 'Child,' she said, 'take a good look at that man on the TV. Look how much you favor him. That man is your father.' Well, I looked at him, looked at him long and hard, looked at him for the better part of thirty minutes until something deep in my soul screamed the loudest scream I've ever felt in my life. That man was my father, the same man they call Minnesota Fats, world's greatest pool shark."

Harvey Fuqua is the world's greatest do-wopper, and Etta's second mentor. As founder of the Moonglows, one of the fifties' premiere vocal groups, Fuqua, like Johnny Otis, is an authentic R&B guru. His harmonic inventions molded the artistic sensibilities of the teenage Marvin Gaye, whom he discovered in Washington, D.C., in 1958. Moreover, Fuqua was a smooth singer himself, and Etta's first lover. He sang on her last track for Modern, "I Hope You're Satisfied." They had also formed a duo under the pseudonyms Betty and Dupree.

"I was this chubby little thing," says Miss James, "I was the original groupie. Thrilled by show biz and all the trappings. I was strung out on Harvey until I was buying the boy rings and hi-fi sets. He was my first love and don't you know I thought he'd be my last. Mercy, was I naive!"

"I appreciated Etta's sense of phrasing, " explains Fuqua, currently lighting director for Smokey Robinson. "Her vocal shadings are more subtle than most people realize, while her feeling is pure dynamite."

"Harvey, " says Etta, "didn't feel nothing for me romantically. He broke my heart. Snapped it in two, that's what he did. Didn't see it coming. What did I know? I was happy being far from home. Happy to be on the chitlin circuit, happy when he took me to Chess Records in Chicago."

By 1960, her period with Modern was over. Her pioneering fifties hits—"The Wallflower" and "Good Rocking Daddy"—along with tunes recorded at Cosimo Matassa's illustrious New Orleans studio—"The Pick Up," "Baby, Baby," "Every Night," "How Big a Fool," and "Market Place"—assure her a place in the early history of the music alongside Ray Charles, Little Richard, and Chuck Berry.

Her move to Chicago had her actually working with Berry, singing backup on "Almost Grown" and "Back in the U.S.A." At Chess she was surrounded by a stable of artists who would reinforce her identity as an uncompromising singer of modern blues. These were country pickers turned big-city belters, masters like Bo Diddley, Muddy Waters, Howlin' Wolf, Willie Dixon, and Little Walter. For the next dozen years, James would soar to the top and crash

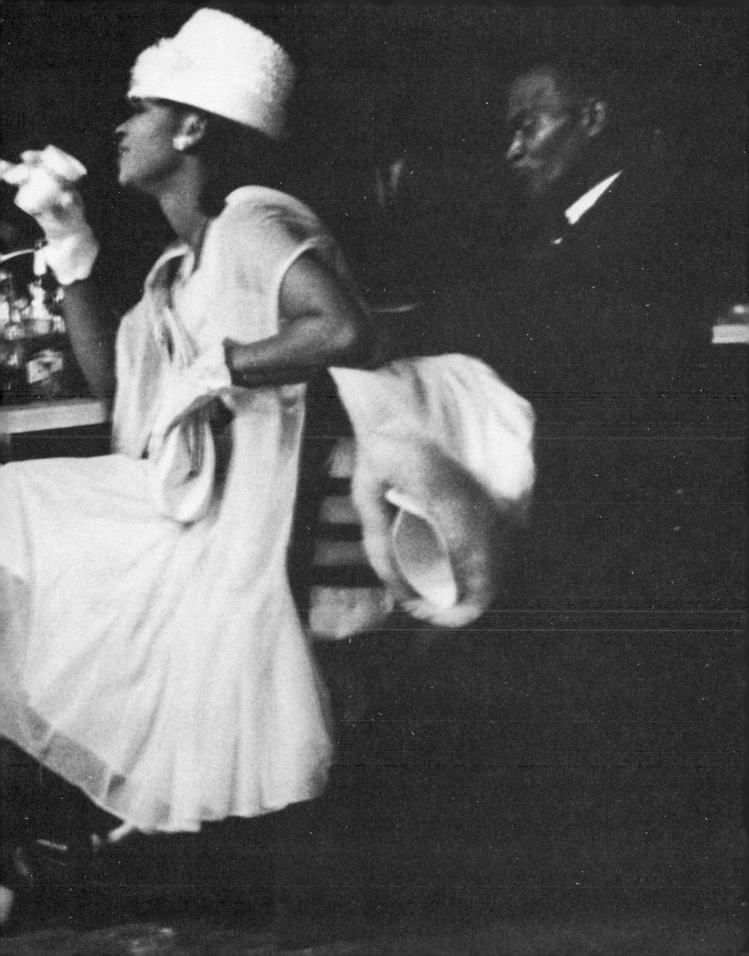

to the bottom, moving from adulation to addiction, back and forth, high and low, determined, desperate, her music the reflection of her struggle.

"Harvey dumped me," she remembers, "and it was especially weird the way it happened. He took Marvin Gaye and jumped over to Detroit where he married one of Berry Gordy's sisters, Gwen, while Marvin married another sister, Anna. Harvey was a sure enough wheeler-dealer. Now the spooky part is that the first hit I had on Chess, "All I Could Do Was Cry," was about a woman who watches her man marry someone else. You know who cowrote that song? Gwen Gordy."

It was also at Chess where Etta evolved into an exquisite interpreter of soul ballads. Her soft jazz-tinged readings of "Trust In Me" and "At Last," for example, are classics, enduring tributes to her most dominant influence.

"Dinah Washington," says Etta through a smile, "was the one. Dinah was the queen. Billie's finesse and feeling are miracles, but it's Dinah's sound, Dinah's chops, Dinah's pride in enunciation and execution, Dinah who did the teaching. Her every musical value was correct. She was church, she was down, she was sweet and salty, she was everything at once. I knew she was trickin', I knew she was really a blues singer, but she was always right, even when she sang pop; she could bend any material into her own gorgeous shape.

"I once met Dinah out on the road. I was still young and, like a fool, I sang one of her hits, "Unforgettable." Afterward she came back, full of scorn, and said to me, 'Girl, don't you ever pull shit like that, not when I'm around.' I burst out in tears. She saw how much she hurt me, so she waited a few minutes before putting her arm around me, saying, 'Child, this is a lesson. Learn it once and you won't have to learn it again.'

"When it comes learning lessons, though, I can be slow. I can be willful and stubborn. I spent so many of my years at Chess just sitting in the back of a limo shooting dope. For a long time I had an attitude with the owner, Leonard Chess. I've called myself a 'Chess slave' and to this day I know the money was funny and the royalties never right. Hell, there weren't any royalties. But looking back, I see that, in his own way, Leonard took care of me. If I didn't have good sense, he did. He bought me a house in L.A. During bad times, he saved the house, protecting me against myself. He put me in his will. He turned out to be my best friend. At one point Leonard sent me to the detox center in Harvey, Illinois, a black sanatorium where I was treated by Art Tatum's brother, a wonderful physician. That stay surely saved my life."

Etta's life, along with her music, grew increasingly intense. In the fifties, she held her own with the best of the male vocalists. The sixties were no different. Her stomp-down dance smashes of the era—"Something's Got a Hold On Me," "I Prefer You," "Tell Mama," "Security"—rival the power of David Ruffin, Dennis Edwards, Otis Redding, and Wilson Pickett. Her stand-up soul numbers, distinctly southern-fried in flavor, are delicious examples of the best of the black music being served up at the time. It was, in fact, in Rick Hall's Fame Studios in Muscle Shoals, Alabama, the Mecca of sixties R&B, where she recorded the poignant "I'd Rather Go Blind," another open-hearted testimony to lost love.

"I felt as though I lost my father," Etta explains, shaking her head in wonder. "During the course of my life, especially after the birth of my two sons, I wanted to meet this man. I wanted him to acknowledge me. Other people knew the story. Nat 'King' Cole, for example, was writing a column for the *Pittsburgh Courier*—Nat was a fan of mine—where he hinted that Fats was my father. There came a time when I couldn't stand it anymore, when I had to go see him. I looked for him for years and finally learned he was living in the Heritage Hotel in Nashville, so I bought a ticket and flew to Tennessee. I was a mess during the whole trip, my head whirling, my stomach churning, my imagination running wild. Felt like I was going to meet my destiny. Got to the hotel, walked in the lobby and there he was, sitting in a big easy chair.

"I felt him feeling me approach him. It was that mystical. As I walked up on him, he made sure to turn his face. He wanted to give me a side view because that's the angle where I resemble him most. He has these eyes, these serious eyes. He gave me a look, the same sort of look I can give, a look that says, 'Don't get too close.' But I had traveled a long way, I was there, and I stood my ground. I stood right straight in front of him. I swallowed hard, took a deep breath. I said his name.

"Minnesota Fats."

"Etta James."

"That's all he said—'Etta James'—and then he half-smiled, letting me know it was okay to be there. He had this little ol' wanna-be singer with him, this four-foot-four hooker with hair all piled on her head, a nervous chick, a bimbo. But I didn't pay her no mind and neither did he. I felt he wanted to hug me. God knows I wanted to hug him. But I was cool. I kept my distance. I was respectful and he was moved, I know he was, because he invited me up to his room where he showed me his trophies—man, there were dozens of trophies—and his poolsticks with diamonds on the back. When I left, he gave me glossy photographs of himself as a young man, looking sharp and clean, but we never did hug, we never did kiss. He never did say he was my daddy."

On another night in a faraway city, when the lights are dim and the mood mellow, Etta sits on a stool, her hair swirled in a bun at the nape of her neck, and sings "Sunday Kind of Love."

"I do my Sunday dreaming every minute, every hour, every day," she cries softly in a voice reminiscent of the voice Dinah Washington used when, on an August afternoon in 1954, she sang "Crazy He Calls Me,"* a voice, out of character for both Etta and Dinah, echoing Billie Holiday.

"I'm conflicted about this jazz thing," she tells you when the crowd's gone and the club's empty. "Sometimes I feel intimidated by great jazz divas like Carmen McRae. Other times I know I have the jazz feeling inside me. When I sing 'Sunday Kind of Love'—and I sing it almost every night—I feel like I'm singing it for Billie, or my mother, or for both of them. It's my way of reaching back and connecting. I need that connection. I hunger for that approval. Without it, I'm back on the streets.

"For awhile, I stayed on the streets. This heroin played rough with me. I had the jones for fourteen years. Barely survived tetanus and lockjaw in Chicago. Became a street junkie in New York. Got caught passing bad checks in California. Just wouldn't do right. And even when a right thing did come along, I had a way of wronging it.

"Take Artis Mills. I met him in Anchorage in 1969. He was this beautiful brother, a young stallion, all fine at six-feet-four and 210 pounds. We fell in love, got married, and then got busted. But Artis, being a gentleman and beautiful soul, took the rap for me. He went to Huntsville prison in Texas. He was there from '71 to '78, and when he got out he came looking for me. I'd been in rehab in Tarzana, California—I was in the psychiatric hospital there close to two years— and had worked through all kinds of therapy. I was another person. My personal life was all changed over. When Artis caught up with me at a show, I didn't know

*This Dinah Washington cut available on two CD reissues: Dinah Jams (EmArcy/PolyGram) and Clifford Brown All Stars, Jams 2 (EmArcy/PolyGram)

whether to break and run or hide and go blind. But you know what? He wasn't angry. He was loving. He'd been waiting all that time to get back with me. It was like a fairy tale come true. The best thing is that we're still together. How did we ever survive?"

While Etta barely survived the seventies, some of her music from that decade remains her most enduring. Her 1973 album, *Etta James*, produced by Gabriel Mekler, challenges her with three ironic Randy Newman tunes—"Sail Away," "Leave Your Hat On," and "God's Song." Her grit proves the perfect vehicle for Newman's wit, her readings gems of overstatement.

Four years later, she'd be off Chess and working with Jerry Wexler, architect of Aretha Franklin's Atlantic sound.

"I always had eyes to produce Etta," says Wexler from his seaside home in Sarasota, Florida. "Even when she was still on Chess, I cut three sides for free, strictly on spec—that's how badly I wanted her. To me, Etta's the quintessential Earth Mother."

The Warner Brothers album, *Deep in the Night,* was a commercial flop but an artistic triumph. "I wanted to bring her along into somewhat more evolved material," explains Wexler. "But perhaps it was too eclectic. I had her singing Hank Williams, Alice Cooper, Top Ten, Eagles, and traditional gospel."

The church number, Dorothy Love Coates's storytelling masterpiece "Strange Man," has Etta returning to her roots, singing how glad she is that Jesus "stopped by in Alabama…one Tuesday evening…and blessed my soul and gone."

Cooper's "Only Women Bleed" and Kiki Dee's "Sugar on the Floor" also capture the essential James, a woman used but not spent, abused but not defeated, vulnerable but finally, through sheer strength of will, victorious.

For the past dozen years Etta James has sought victory in various places, pursuing the sort of crossover audience captured, say, by her contemporary Tina Turner. But Etta's not Tina, and although James's brand of tough-minded rhythm and blues spawned a whole school of followers, from Janis Joplin to Bonnie Raitt, the arena-rock crowd has never come calling. Aside from a few exceptional venues—opening the 1984 Olympics in Los Angeles, for instance—Etta has steadily built her audience on blues aficionados. Her fare has been been select clubs, medium-sized concerts, and festivals, especially in Europe where the real thing is still revered. Even though she's prospered as a performer, her records have appeared only sporadically—an all-gospel production, tracks with Allen Toussaint, a two-part album with Eddie "Cleanhead" Vinson.

Seven Year Itch, referring to her long recording dearth, was released in 1988 and produced by Muscle Shoals keyboardist Barry Beckett, who brought her back down South, back to Nashville, where he also put together *Stickin' to My Guns*, her first album of the nineties, a reflection of Etta's adamancy about singing sixties soul.

You're on one coast and Etta's calling from another. It's past midnight and the sound of her speaking voice, like her singing, is filled with surprise, her passion for self-exploration still running high.

After singing the praises of the Thunderbirds and Stevie Ray Vaughan—"he's the baddest bluesman out there today"—she turns inward.

"I have this paradox about me. I come on so proud and pushy, so secure. I'll tell you that I'm making more money from appearances than ever before—and that's the truth. I'm cocky. I know I can sing. I give an impression of all this strength. Maybe that's why the Lesbian crowd likes me and the gay boys spill their guts to me. I act like I'm ready to kick anyone's ass who's in my way. Don't want people bugging me, telling me to do this or do that. I'm tough. But I'm not, I swear I'm not.

"I'm an artist with a lot of voices inside my head, some of them scared, some of them sweet, some of them carrying urgent messages. When I sing my brand of blues, or jazz, or rhythm and blues, or whatever the hell they're calling it these days, it's those messages that move me, the messages that come from the gut. Don't you see, the messages are my lifeline to the world. The messages make me carry on."

CHUCK BERRY

BERRYLAND

by Bob Blumenthal

Rock and roll is not the blues—at least not in its entirety—and the same might be said regarding Chuck Berry, the singer/guitarist many consider synonymous with rock and roll. In an attempt to pinpoint what he does in his 1987 *Chuck Berry: The Autobiography*, Berry insisted that "The nature and backbone of my beat is boogie and the muscle of my music is melodies that are simple. Call it what you may: jive, jazz, jump, swing, soul, rhythm, rock, or even punk, it's still boogie so far as I'm connected with it." What about blues, he asks rhetorically? "I dig blues when I'm blue."

A boogie beat and melodies that are simple. In that terse formula, Berry pinpoints the essence of rock as precisely as any scholar, and catalogs the particular strands that solidify the music's blues connection. What Berry's definition omits—rock's knack for addressing its particular audience, and for using the tools of the music business to recast that audience as an international

brotherhood—are the very traits that set Berry apart from his blues predecessors, and lend his example to followers as likely to turn a deaf ear to the blues as to embrace it. If Berry deserves much of the credit (or, depending upon your bias, blame) for the Rolling Stones, the same could be said regarding the Beach Boys.

The diverse reach of his influence only echoes the dichotomies of Berry's own personality. He is both down-home natural and urbane sophisticate, haunted itinerant and market manipulator supreme. His life echoes the romantic legends of numerous blues predecessors, even as his music brought the blues to people and places these elders could barely imagine.

At root, these tensions follow from the circumstances of his childhood. Charles Edward Berry was born in Saint Louis in 1926 and grew up in this not-quite-Northern, not-quite-Southern metropolis. Saint Louis may be on the Mississippi River, but it is not the Delta; and Berry's youth, while circumscribed by societal prejudice as surely as that of any African-American of his generation, was in critical respects not all that removed from the experiences of his future fans. He was the fourth child in a large family where Mom stayed home while Dad provided a modest but steady income as a handyman for a realty company. Music was a central part of his experience, from the gospel tunes his mother played on the family piano to the popular race records his brothers and sisters would sneak into the house. He started to sing, raising eyebrows when he performed the Walter Brown/Jay McShann hit "Confessin' the Blues" at the 1941 Sumner High School student show, and learned the rudiments of guitar playing from friends and neighbors on a four-stringed instrument; but he had other interests as well. He loved photography, and installed a darkroom in the family basement prior to entering high school; and, around 1943, he satisfied another passion by purchasing the first of many cars.

Driving his car to high school, where he was an active member of the photography club, Berry was an unlikely blues master of the future. Yet his hot-rodding, fast-living adolescence anticipated the experiences that white suburban teens would appropriate a decade later. Berry's ability to capture these activities (they were, after all, so close to his own) explains much about his popularity. At the same time, Berry was a black teenager, and when he stepped out of line, there were no second chances. A joyride to Kansas City with two buddies in 1944 turned into a wayward adventure involving armed robbery and a stolen car. Berry received nearly three years in the Algoa Intermediate Reformatory for Young Men for his indiscretion. It would not be his last confinement.

The years in Algoa, where Berry boxed and sang in a vocal quartet, and those that immediately followed his release late in 1947 conform most closely to the standard blues mythology. Shortly after returning to Saint Louis, he married Themetta "Toddy" Suggs, had the first of his children, and committed the first of many infidelities. He worked janitorial jobs with his father and at the Fisher auto body assembly plant, and played one-night stands at clubs and parties when he could find a gig. While not yet committed to music, Berry was already ambitious. In 1950 he purchased a small house and a television; the following summer he bought a wire recorder and began setting down what he describes as "the first of my original improvisations, both poetical and melodical."

It was at this point that music began to take over. Now armed with a six-string guitar, Berry began to spend time with Ira Harris, a neighborhood guitarist who favored jazz and played in a style Berry describes as similar to that of electric guitar pioneer Charlie Christian. "Ira showed me many licks and riffs on the guitar that came to be the foundation of the style that is said to be Chuck Berry's," he admits. Another acknowledged influence was Carl Hogan, the guitarist with Louis Jordan's Tympany Five. Saxophonist/vocalist Jordan (1908–1975) led one of the most popular blues combos of the forties, a group known for its clever, humorous lyrics and pervasive showmanship, characteristics that would also be critical to Berry's success. T-Bone Walker and Elmore James also left their marks on Berry's playing. In regard to what younger white fans began to call the Chuck Berry style, Berry is honest enough to confess that "there is nothing new under the sun."

What Berry did achieve in his playing was both a variation on his idols and a broader synthesis of the diverse music heard in his environment. He was a most receptive lightning rod for these various impulses, particularly after he began working regularly with the guitarist Tommy Stevens's combo in 1952, and then pianist Johnny Johnson's Sir John's Trio the following year. As local bar bands, these groups were called upon to reproduce the popular music of the day—Muddy Waters, Elmore James, and Joe Turner on the blues side, the ballads of Nat Cole for romantic contrast, and even the Caribbean exotica of Harry Belafonte. There was also country-western music everywhere, which Berry had the temerity to work into his act. Soon he became known as the "black hillbilly," a performer with flamboyant gestures (including the stooped but stiffbacked duck walk he developed as a child) and a keen musical empathy with his fellow players, especially Johnson. Already, Berry was taking the measure of his audience. "Listening to my idol Nat Cole prompted me to sing sentimental songs with distinct diction. The songs of

Chuck Berry

Muddy Waters impelled me to deliver the down-home blues in the language they come from, Negro dialect. When I played hillbilly songs, I stressed my diction so that it was harder and whiter. All in all it was my intention to hold both the black and the white clientele by voicing the different kinds of songs in their customary tongues."

So Berry was more than ready in 1955 when he sought out Muddy Waters on a trip to Chicago and was directed to Leonard Chess of Chess Records. His recording sessions from that year catalog his sources as well as his uniqueness. There were the relatively familiar blues strains of "Wee Wee Hours," inspired by Joe Turner's "Wee Baby Blues," and "No Money Down," with its break figures in the verse so reminiscent of Waters; and there was the seductive blues balladry of "Together We Will Always Be." Something else was going on, though, in "Maybelline," "Thirty Days," and "You Can't Catch Me." These numbers were blues-derived from a structural and harmonic standpoint, and the note-riding and slurred chords on "Maybelline's" guitar solo clearly echoed T-Bone Walker and other models. Still, these were blues with a difference. The lyrics carried sophisticated wordplay and timely references in their sagas of motorvatin' airmobiles. Arranging touches that would soon become trademarks appeared, like the tinkling Otis Spann piano on "You Can't Catch Me." Most unusual of all was that emphatic, foot-stomping rhythm, the black hillbilly edge developed in Saint Louis. It was as if Berry had emerged from his own darkroom, a photographic negative image of the hillbilly/blues fusion a young man named Presley was developing in a Memphis recording studio at around the same time.

Berry clearly had more to learn; but most of his remaining lessons concerned the tricks of the music business and the nature of his audience. "Maybelline," his first hit from his first session, was originally known as "Ida May" and had been derived quite obviously from "Ida Red," a country song recorded by Bob Wills and Cowboy Copas among others. Change the title, Leonard Chess had insisted, and you can claim composer royalties. Berry got the point, particularly after "Maybelline" was published and disc jockey Alan Freed and a third man were listed as cocomposers. There were other insights gained when Berry began to tour in late 1955, including the skimming of the manager assigned to his first East Coast swing and the unreliability of pianist Johnson and drummer Ebby Harding, who were now his sidemen. Ever the practical, security conscious planner, Berry began to do his own business. He bought a tour bus on his first visit to California, then left it in Missouri upon realizing that traveling as a single and working with pickup rhythm sections meant more money and fewer headaches. Soon Francine

Gillium, a fan from Pittsburgh and one of many women to figure in Berry's life, had moved to Saint Louis and began to oversee the day-to-day details of what was becoming Berry's empire.

An equally invaluable revelation concerned just who Berry's fans were. His first appearance at the Paramount Theater in New York suggested what a subsequent tour of the South confirmed: white teenagers were drawn to his music, and in substantial numbers. Leonard Chess had been right— "Wee Wee Hours" might appeal to the rhythm and blues crowd, but the flip side, "Maybelline," would be a "pop" (i.e., white) phenomenon. This was a lesson to take to the bank.

Over the course of 1956, Berry pulled the diverse strands of his music together. There were the lyrical refinements of a more traditional blues like "Too Much Monkey Business," equal parts homemade syntax ("botheration") and unlikely allusion ("my objection's overruled"); the Tex-Mex lope of "Brown-Eyed Handsome Man"; and the lingering Nat Cole vignettes in "Havana Moon." It was "Roll Over, Beethoven," though, where Berry first made an overt pitch to his newfound fans; and "School Days," recorded nearly a year later, where the narrative slant and emphatic boogie rhythms approached their ultimate refinement. "Beethoven" found Berry introducing his insistent, T-Bone-style opening guitar chorus and ringing solos, while the rhythm section (in this case Johnson, bassist Willie Dixon, and drummer Fred Below) refined the hard backbeat groove. It was also on "Beethoven" that Berry's lyrics first agglomerated the everyday references of teen life (the local deejay, the Rhythm Revue, blue suede shoes) with nursery rhymes and more highfallutin' references in a manner that his audience found as comfortable as it was revelatory. "School Days" brought the lyrics and the music into more perfect balance, as Berry's memories of "practical math," "the cook in the lunchroom," and the after-school "juke joint" were answered by rumbling guitar riffs, all culminating in the declaration "Hail, hail rock and roll." Sumner High School, circa 1943, had met the suburban high of the fifties.

Buoyed by the success of "School Days," his second single to crack the pop top ten, Berry wasted no time applying his now-finished conception. Beginning in May of 1957, with the more flamboyant Lafayette Leake replacing Johnson on piano and stalwarts Dixon and Below completing the rhythm section, he launched the most productive and successful period of his career. Every song was a paean to rock and its fans—"Oh Baby Doll," the school-is-out sequel to his big hit; "Reelin' and Rockin'," inspired by teenage memories of Joe Turner at the

Rum Boogie, translated (with the help of Leake's Jerry Lee Lewis–style piano) to a more contemporary dancehall; "Around and Around," another sock-hop scene with a vocal that had an especially strong impact on Mick Jagger. Three other titles cut with Leake, Dixon, and Below proved to be definitive. "Rock and Roll Music," with its atmospheric narrative of trips across the tracks and jamborees, extolled the genre with the unshakeable backbeat; "Johnny B. Goode" glorified the genre's hero, a rags-to-riches type modeled on his creator with liberal embellishments (Johnny was a country boy from around New Orleans, rather than a colored boy from Saint Louis), who gained success through the lure of his guitar; and "Sweet Little Sixteen," the prototype fan with the "grown-up blues" who was caught in the madness of the music as her counterparts were all over the country. The ringing chords and staccato breaks were still present, together with familiar blues structures; but these blues were informed by the sensibility of the 45-rpm single, and the new means for its promotion. Berry had become a regular visitor to Dick Clark's daily and nighttime programs, and appreciated how television was already magnifying his impact. When it came time to inventory the places where Sweet Little Sixteen danced, Berry made sure to note that she was "rockin' on Bandstand."

Johnny Johnson,

Berry's longtime pianist.

Often overlooked, his

playing with Berry

helped invent rock and

roll style piano.

      Berry's output remained inspired into early 1959, even after Johnson had returned as his studio pianist. "Carol," "Sweet Little Rock and Roller," and "Little Queenie" kept the theme of the idealized female rocker fresh, thanks in large measure to the urgency of Berry's guitar and the clever conceits of his lyrics. One song from this period, "Memphis," was darker and more haunting, with an ominous instrumental track (Berry claims to have overdubbed all of the parts himself in his office/studio) and an especially poignant narrative about the singer's estranged six-year-old daughter who was last seen "with hurry-home drops on her cheeks." "Almost Grown," from early in 1959, should have been another milestone, with its typically sly lyrics acknowledging that there would be more to life than high school; yet its souped-up mix, with Johnson pounding his piano fills into clichés and the Moonglows adding vocal support that nearly smothered the band, actually signaled more blatant calculations. Chuck Berry style was growing routine; the golden era was ending.

      For a time, Berry was able to capitalize on his success and become something of an entrepreneur in his hometown. He purchased thirty acres in the nearby countryside in 1957, then turned it into the recreation center Berry Park three years later. Club Bandstand, an integrated nightspot, opened in Saint Louis in 1958 and operated for two years. Romantic indiscretions were soon to catch up with Berry, though to this day he protests his innocence. Toward the end

Chuck Berry

of 1959, he was arrested for transporting a female Native American minor from Texas to Missouri in violation of the Mann Act. An earlier episode resurfaced, in which Berry had been arrested while traveling with a young French woman and carrying a concealed weapon. Three trials followed over the next two years, and Berry's career began to fall apart. He continued to record, but an occasional convincing performance (such as "Down the Road Apiece") could not disguise that most of the results were throwaways, Berry going through the motions in order to pay his legal bills. Early in 1962 he was back in jail, serving nearly two years in the Federal Medical Center at Springfield, Missouri.

Proving to be nothing if not resilient, Berry emerged from prison in a burst of creative energy. The music he recorded in early 1964 did not veer far from his norm beyond the presence of a sax section, but was pungent

and clever like the Berry of old. "No Particular Place to Go" and "Promised Land" offered fresh views on old themes; "You Never Can Tell," recounting a surprisingly successful domestic scene, seemed to complete a coming-of-age trilogy begun by "School Days" and "Almost Grown"; and "Nadine," with the singer "campaign shoutin' like a Southern diplomat" in pursuit of his elusive lover, introduced one of his most memorable females. Berry still had the market cornered on lucid, intelligent rock lyrics, and for the moment his music was equally crisp.

His comeback could not have taken place at a more auspicious time. The Beatles, the Rolling Stones, and other British groups had begun to crack the American market and were making clear, through their comments and numerous cover versions, that Chuck Berry was a primary inspiration. Suddenly he was a living legend, back on the television rock shows and the concert circuit, a godfather to the superstars of the day.

As it turns out, though, Berry, not yet forty, was at the end of his creative road. He seized upon his reborn fame only to become a fixture on the oldies circuit, endlessly reprising his hits while recording inferior remakes under a new recording contract. His ability to sustain his status as a rock pioneer, culminating in the film that documented his sixtieth birthday concert, *Hail! Hail! Rock 'n' Roll*, has been his most impressive achievement in the past twenty-five years. That he had his biggest-selling single in 1972 with the smutty frat-house favorite "My Ding-A-Ling" is only ironic.

Further brushes with the law are primarily responsible for keeping Chuck Berry in the public eye in recent decades. After several years of investigating his financial dealings, the IRS finally convicted him of tax evasion in 1979. Into the Lompoc, California, penitentiary he went for four months, his third trip to the slammer. Noting that his incarcerations occurred at seventeen-year intervals, Berry comments near the end of his autobiography that "My next fall is due around year end of 1996," though this may prove to be wishful thinking. As the nineties arrived, he was in trouble again, this time for pornographic photos he had taken (with or without the consent of the models, depending upon whom you believed). High-priced lawyers went on talk shows to cite the First Amendment and explain that the pictures had only been shot for the singer's "personal use," while pictures of "Chuck Berry Nude!" were suddenly hyped in bold headlines on the covers of the less reputable men's magazines. It appeared that Chuck Berry might be more the prototypical bluesman than even he suspected, succumbing to that oldest of hellhounds that not even a cool breeze can outrun.

Chuck Berry,

Chess Studios, Chicago.

(facing page)

ACKNOWLEDGMENTS

In addition to all the contributors to this book, special thanks goes to three people in particular who contributed greatly to this book and remained committed throughout trying to secure a publisher and the long process of bringing this book to life.

In the beginning, Rick Saylor, my partner (and close friend and I grew up together listening to the same music and reading many of the same writings and who was always on his way to the city to catch B. B. or Albert or some giant) in the production of this book contributed more than anyone. His suggestions, passions and astute editorial judgment helped to *finally* get it to press. Helen Oakely Dance suggested the title and has been a *major* inspiration throughout; Pete Welding, I can't thank and appreciate enough! First, In the 1960s, I read with voracity his voluminous writings on the blues on record album notes, *downbeat* issues and many sundry articles and essays he published during those times. Pete's knowledge, insights, and deep feeling are unsurpassed. From the beginning, he was a major booster in the making of this book and contributed a great deal of time, thought and effort with ideas, observations and comments as to how the different elements of the book would work best.

Additionally, there are many others who've contributed to this book along the way and helped round out the collection: Peter Guralnick, Paul DeAngelis, Gary Luke, Mack McCormick, The Living Blues Archive at Oxford, Mississippi; Andy McKaie and Gary Chansley at MCA Records, Colin Escott, Dave Booth, Elektra Records, Art Fine, Kirk Silsbee, Ray Flerlage, Chris Albertson, Val Wilmer, Frank Driggs, Alan Govenar, Ray Avery and Bonner Beuhler.

Kudos to Eric Baker Design Associates—Eric Baker, Susi Oberhelman, Patrick Seymour, Michael Ross and Karen Alban Blankenship (and Bonnie Resnick Baker!). Also to Neal Stuart, Blair Fraser and Maggie Payette at Dutton.

My deep appreciation goes out to Kevin Mulroy, our editor, who stood by this book through thick and thin (and postponements) yet always pushed forward.

Special thanks must go to a cast of characters (some forgotten) from a long time ago—Bob Webb, Stanley Jackson, Lonnie Walters, Fast Eddie, Harry Duncan, Steve Byron, Willie Smith, Cat and everyone who ever did the door for us at Mr. Lee's (1-2-3 look at…).

And thanks to Albert Murray for "Stompin' The Blues."

T.R.B.

Photographs by Ray Avery: pages 84, 112, 153, 222.

Photographs by William Claxton: pages 150, 156, 162-163, 170-171.

Photographs by Ray Flerlage: pages 49, 92-93, 125, 140-141, 145, 146, 149, 155, 166, 167, 177, 190, 199, 201, 208-209, 214-215, 230-231, 254-255.

Photograph by Hooks Brothers: page 187.

Photograph by Charles Nadell: page 186.

Photographs by Val Wilmer: pages 9, 108, 137, 212.

Photograph by Ernest C. Withers: page 202.

Photograph courtesy of Chris Albertson: page 51.

Photographs courtesy of Avalon Archives: pages 17, 54, 66, 105, 120, 121, 191, 205.

Photographs courtesy of Frank Driggs collection: pages 36, 39, 45, 48-49, 58, 59, 63, 79, 83, 99, 100, 128, 186, 239.

Photograph courtesy of Elektra Records: page 246.

Photographs courtesy of Alan Govenar: pages 19, 25, 26, 30, 37.

Photographs courtesy of Professor Longhair Foundation: page 159.

Photographs courtesy of MCA Records: pages 132, 219, 225, 235, 242-243.

Photographs courtesy of Showtime Music Archive: pages 115, 131, 135, 142, 144, 148, 156, 178, 183, 185, 192, 228, 229, 247, 248.

Photographs courtesy of Texas/Dallas History and Archives Division, Dallas Public Library: pages 18, 20-21, 32-33.